THE GENERALISATION OF THE
GENERAL THEORY

THE GENERALISATION OF THE GENERAL THEORY

AND OTHER ESSAYS

BY

JOAN ROBINSON

ST. MARTIN'S PRESS
NEW YORK

First edition 1952 as *The Rate of Interest and Other Essays*
Second edition 1979 as *The Generalisation of the General
Theory and Other Essays*

All rights reserved. For further information write:
St. Martin's Press, Inc., 175 Fifth Avenue, New York, NY 10010
Printed in Great Britain
First published in the United States of America in 1979

ISBN 0-312-31963-0

Library of Congress Cataloging in Publication Data

Robinson, Joan, 1903–
   The generalisation of the general theory, and other
essays.

   First ed. published in 1952 under title: The rate
of interest, and other essays.
      1. Econimics. 2. Keynes, John Maynard, 1883–1946.
The general theory of employment, interest and money.
3. Technological innovations. 4. Interest and usury.
5. Statics and dynamics (Social sciences) I. Title.
HB171.R644 1979b   330.1   79-15275
ISBN 0-312 31963-0

CONTENTS

CONTENTS

PREFACE

This book consists of a reprint of *The Rate of Interest and Other Essays* (published in 1952) with the order reversed and a new introduction.

The essay on the Rate of Interest appeared in *Econometrica* (April 1951) and is republished here with the kind permission of the Editor. It was reprinted, along with some small excerpts from this book, in *Collected Economic Papers* Vol. II, Blackwells, Oxford.

INTRODUCTION — 1978

The "habitual modes of thought and expression" from which Keynes had "a long struggle to escape" in writing the *General Theory of Employment Interest and Money* were derived in the main from Alfred Marshall. When I was writing these essays four or five years after the end of the war, I was taking it for granted that the escape had been made; I was aiming to carry the modes of thought and expression of the General Theory into new fields, in particular, following Harrod, into the analysis of accumulation and growth. I wrote in the introduction to the first edition of this book:

The theme of these essays is the analysis of a dynamic economic system. The characteristic of a dynamic analysis, in the sense intended here, is that it cannot explain how an economy behaves, in given conditions, without reference to past history; while static analysis purports to describe a position of equilibrium which the system will reach (or would reach if the given conditions remained unchanged for long enough) no matter where it started from.

Short-period analysis is concerned with the equilibrium of a system with a given stock of capital and with given expectations about the future. Past history is thus put into the initial conditions, so that the analysis is static in itself, and yet is part of a dynamic theory. (This explains the paradox that although Keynes' *General Theory* is strictly static in form, it has opened the way for a great outburst of analysis of dynamic problems.)

We have all been studying dynamic economics all our lives, for no one can refrain from reflecting, from time to time, on actual economic events, and actual events are always dynamic. Only in the sealed vacuum of the classrooms where equilibrium theory is taught can static problems be discussed, and even there the outside air is always leaking in. Most of the results of the following analysis are therefore obvious and familiar. It seems, however, worth while to try to connect the familiar problems with the classroom analysis, for so long as the analysis is static and the problems dynamic the two are for ever at cross-purposes.

A short stage in the process of connection is all that I can offer. The level of abstraction maintained in the following argument is very high. In particular it is conducted in terms of a single economy (there is no discussion of international trade) and it is conducted almost entirely in terms of global conceptions such as "total output" and "total employment", paying no attention (except at a few points) to qualitative differences between commodities, types of labour, etc.

I offer the argument at this primitive stage as an agenda for discussion, rather than as a completed piece of analysis. Having grown up swaddled in equilibrium theory I find my muscles soft, and to venture into dynamic problems induces a tendency to vertigo. Since there may be others in like case, I feel it is worth the attempt to clear up some very simple problems, in the hope that our heads may grow stronger as we go on.

Meanwhile a different style of teaching swamped the tradition of Marshall, distorted Keynes and failed to follow the dynamic clue, so that the struggle to escape has now to be more strenuous than ever.

Micro-macro Theories

In the modern textbooks there is a dichotomy between micro and macro departments which is alien to the General Theory. In Marshall there was compartmentalisation, which Keynes broke down, between "real" and "monetary" problems, but not between global relationships and individual behaviour. There cannot be a macro theory of employment and income in the economy as a whole without a micro picture of its structure—industry, commerce, banking—and of the motives and decisions of its inhabitants: financiers, managers, workers, professionals and housewives. Keynes used global concepts to hack out a new path through the tangle of old doctrines, but he did not intend them to be understood as simple quantities. When he defined aggregate demand as "the proceeds which entrepreneurs expect to receive" from the product of a certain level of employment, he was concerned with the views of individuals and groups appraising the situation in a complex inter-related pattern of businesses, markets and industries, not with a mere number of millions of pounds sterling. When the global lines had been laid out, a great deal of detail remained to be filled in. In this, the latter-day micro theories have been no help.

There are two branches of textbook micro theory, not always kept sufficiently distinct. One branch broke completely with Marshall and looked for inspiration to Walras. Here, there is no structure of the economy but a mass of anonymous transactors meeting in a competitive market. Its internal operations are not easy to understand, for individuals in their capacity as sellers have to decide what commodities to offer while in their capacity as buyers they are choosing (according to taste) amongst supplies of products already in existence. It works best in the famous case of the prisoner-of-war camp where ready-made goods arrive in Red Cross parcels. Alternatively, it can be applied to a village fair in an economy of what Marx called simple commodity production, though I found when I tried to work it out[1] that textbook propositions are not always valid. In any case, neither type of market can be fitted into a treatment of production and distribution in a capitalist economy. The attempt to graft Keynes on to Walras has led to great confusion.[2]

The other branch of textbook theory was derived from Marshall but in the highly formalised version propagated by Pigou, which entirely eliminates the dynamic element from it. (Keynes took Pigou as the principle representative of the school of thought from which he was struggling to escape.) Here there are individual firms each producing a rate of output such that marginal cost is equal to price, provided that price is not less than average cost. Thus any firm which is producing at all is working up to capacity and the rest are in mothballs. My *Imperfect Competition* modified this picture, but unfortunately it was not really much of an improvement.

When price exceeds average cost the firm is making more than normal profits, which will attract new competition into the market. Instead of seizing the opportunity while it lasts to make investments and consolidate its competitive position, the firm tamely allows itself, "in the long run", to be pushed back to its equilibrium level of output at minimum average cost.

The costs of the firm include interest on the value of the capital (equipment and stocks) that it is operating.

---

[1] *Exercises in Economic Analysis*, Part Three.

[2] Axel Leijonhufvud has repudiated this attempt and returned to the Marshallian tradition; see "Keynes' Employment Function" (comment) *History of Political Economy*, Vol. 6, 1974.

For Pigou, interest was not a monetary phenomenon but the source of rentier income—the reward of waiting. In the ultimate stationary state, where accumulation has come to an end, there is a schedule relating the rate of interest to the stock of wealth that rentiers are willing to own. (If the return were higher they would be saving and, if lower, consuming capital.) In equilibrium, the rate of profit on capital is equal to the rate of interest. This determines the number of firms (each of equilibrium size), the technique of production and the level of real wages.

I believe that it was a vague memory of this concept of long-run equilibrium that lay behind the confusion between financial wealth receiving interest and physical capital earning profits in the neo-neoclassical conception of accumulation.

My challenge—I leave those who draw production functions to say what marginal productivity and the elasticity of substitution mean when labour and capital are the factors of production[3]—was never taken up and the great "capital" controversy of the 1960s was never resolved. The neo-neoclassicals abandoned the field and retreated, behind a smoke screen of algebra, into a world where somehow the future has already happened.

Textbook teaching in the department of so-called macro theory was an attempt to push Keynes into short-period equilibrium. The IS/LM diagram of J. R. Hicks seems to show the level of income and employment as a simple decreasing function of the rate of interest. This leaves out three of the main elements in the *General Theory*: the dependence of investment upon expectations of future profits, the distinction between real and money income, according to the level of money-wage rates and

[3] See p. 102 below.

the ability of the authorities to increase the quantity of money (moving LM to the right) when employment is restricted by lack of finance. Keynes pointed this out at the time;[4] although Sir John Hicks has now repudiated IS/LM, he still does not seem to have understood Keynes' letter.[5]

The grand neoclassical synthesis (now known as bastard Keynesism) was a more ambitious attempt to reduce the General Theory to a system of equilibrium. At any moment, in a particular country, there is a particular overall rate of saving that would be realised at full employment. The authorities by fiscal and monetary policy must ensure that the level of home investment and the foreign balance are such as to absorb this rate of saving. Then equilibrium growth will be continuously realised.

In the era of stagflation, this notion has been discredited and the quantity theory of money is blossoming afresh amongst its ruins.

HISTORY *versus* EQUILIBRIUM

It was precisely from the concept of equilibrium that Keynes was struggling to escape. As he was concerned to account for an actual phenomenon—unemployment—in an actual economy—contemporary capitalism—he had to discuss it in terms of processes taking place in actual history. The concept of equilibrium is incompatible with history. It is a metaphor based on movements in space applied to processes taking place in time. In space, it is possible to go to and fro and remedy misdirections, but in time, every day, the past is irrevocable and the future unknown. When bodies are out of balance with

4 J.M.K., Vol. XIV. pp. 79-81.
5 See *Economic Perspectives*, Oxford 1977, p. viii.

each other in space, given time, they can move towards equilibrium. "Time will help you with space, but take as much space as you like—how is that going to help you with time?"[6]

Keynes was naturally trying to set out his argument in historical time, but he did not see quite clearly what he had been doing till after the book was published. In "The General Theory of Employment" 1937[7] he explained what an essential part was played by the uncertainty of the future in his scheme of ideas.

By "uncertain" knowledge, let me explain, I do not mean merely to distinguish what is known for certain from what is only probable. The game of roulette is not subject, in this sense, to uncertainty; nor is the prospect of a Victory bond being drawn. Or, again, the expectation of life is only slightly uncertain. Even the weather is only moderately uncertain. The sense in which I am using the term is that in which the prospect of a European war is uncertain, or the price of copper and the rate of interest twenty years hence, or the obsolescence of a new invention, or the position of private wealth owners in the social system in 1970. About these matters there is no scientific basis on which to form any calculable probability whatever. We simply do not know. Nevertheless, the necessity for action and for decision compels us as practical men to do our best to overlook this awkward fact and to behave exactly as we should if we had behind us a good Benthamite calculation of a series of prospective advantages and disadvantages,

6 "A Lecture Delivered at Oxford by a Cambridge Economist", 1951. Reprinted in *Collected Economic Papers*, Vol. IV.

7 J.M.K., Vol. XIV, p. 109 *et seq.*

each multiplied by its appropriate probability, waiting to be summed.[8]

Though this is how we behave in the market place, the theory we devise in the study of how we behave in the market place should not itself submit to market-place idols. I accuse the classical economic theory of being itself one of these pretty, polite techniques which tries to deal with the present by abstracting from the fact that we know very little about the future.

I daresay that a classical economist[9] would readily admit this. But, even so, I think he has overlooked the precise nature of the difference which his abstraction makes between theory and practice, and the character of the fallacies into which he is likely to be led.[10]

It was for this reason that Keynes made little use of the kind of mathematical formalism which is so fashionable nowadays. He was discussing relationships that cannot be reduced to a system of axioms.

The object of our analysis is, not to provide a machine, or method of blind manipulation, which will furnish an infallible answer, but to provide ourselves with an organised and orderly method of thinking out particular problems; and, after we have reached a provisional conclusion by isolating the complicating factors one by one, we then have to go back on ourselves and allow, as well as we can, for the probable interactions of the factors amongst themselves. This is the

[8] Ibid., pp. 113-14

[9] Keynes habitually used "classical" to cover everyone from Ricardo to Pigou.

[10] J.M.K., Vol. XIV, p. 115

nature of economic thinking. Any other way of applying our formal principles of thought (without which, however, we shall be lost in the wood) will lead us into error. It is a great fault of symbolic pseudo-mathematical methods of formalising a system of economic analysis that they expressly assume strict independence between the factors involved and lose all their cogency and authority if this hypothesis is disallowed; whereas, in ordinary discourse, where we are not blindly manipulating but know all the time what we are doing and what the words mean, we can keep "at the back of our heads" the necessary reserves and qualifications and the adjustments which we shall have to make later on, in a way in which we cannot keep complicated partial differentials "at the back" of several pages of algebra which assume that they all vanish. Too large a proportion of recent "mathematical" economics are mere concoctions, as imprecise as the inital assumptions they rest on, which allow the author to lose sight of the complexities and interdependencies of the real world in a maze of pretentious and unhelpful symbols.[11]

My generalisation of the General Theory was an attempt to treat the analysis of accumulation according to Keynes' prescription. I worked out the internal relationships of a capitalist economy in steady growth—a golden age—omitting the large fields of foreign trade and government action which, however, are susceptible to be treated in the same manner. I used it as the background to analyse departures from it—that is to study the effect upon a growing economy of various types of vicissitudes that it may meet with. This propounds no doctrines but maps out a large area of the problems that

[11] *General Theory*, pp. 297-8.

should be investigated in the light of contemporary history. I still believe that something on these lines is a necessary preparation for "applying our formal principles of thought" to economic reality, but most of the profession seems to prefer the methods described in the last lines of the above quotation.

LIMITS TO GROWTH

One type of vicissitude, now topical, which I did not discuss is the depletion of specific natural resources, as opposed to scarcity of "land" in general.

There seems to be a good deal of confusion in public discussion between the apprehension that the growth of industry in the future will be brought to a halt by the exhaustion of sources of materials (especially fossil fuels) and the experience of a sharp decline in growth with the slump of 1974. It is true that the slump was precipitated (not caused) by the oil crisis, but this was not due to a reduction in specific supplies but to a contraction in world-wide effective demand with the sudden jump in unspent profits of OPEC and the oil companies. There was also an indirect effect. The rise in prices of oil, and of other materials that set in even before 1974, exacerbated inflation in the industrial countries which led to the imposition of financial restrictions and to the spread of the political doctrine that unemployment is the lesser evil.

So long as the slump lasts, demand for materials is deficient, scarcities disappear and the terms of trade swing back in favour of industry.

In itself, the threat of long-run scarcities is not a cause of depression but the reverse. It provides a motive for investment in alternative sources of supply, installing more economic methods of production and adaptation of the means of consumption to less extravagant forms. A deterioration of the terms of trade, foreseen in good time, should be the basis of a long boom in investment. But the doctrine that the free play of market forces allocates scarce means, in a rational manner, between alternative uses needs to be thoroughly well overhauled from the macro top to the micro bottom.

Behind this lies a deeper question—what is it that we want to grow? Capital accumulation is now controlled mainly by the military–industrial complexes of many countries (both advanced and underdeveloped) and the plans of the great trans-national corporations. They find themselves with excess capacity in many lines, but trade unions, governments and the general public are begging them to invest in something, in anything, in order to increase employment. It is an illusion that the private-enterprise system is highly flexible. It is stuck in rigid grooves and can give employment only by pushing further down them.

Keynes' view was that if income were less unequally distributed, consumption would be a higher proportion of full-employment income and there would be less need for investment to fill the gap.

This is certainly true in the Third World. If the now miserable urban and rural population had more to eat, they would buy simple old-fashioned goods—shirts and shoes and saucepans—that can be produced by small-scale capital-saving methods. In wealthy countries, if advertisement ceased to create wants, leisure and education might be preferred to shopping.

J. K. Galbraith has argued strongly on this side of the question, but he believes in the power of educated public opinion to influence the great corporations to follow humane and enlightened policies. Meanwhile, it is they who have the power to educate the public to demand what they find it profitable to supply and to vote for administrations that will not jeopardise their power to do so.

The Rate of Profit

There is a serious awkwardness in the theoretical scheme underlying my first attempt to generalise the General Theory, which was undertaken before we had the benefit of Piero Sraffa's re-interpretation of Ricardo; it lacked a coherent concept of the rate of profit on capital.

First of all I was using a clumsy terminology. I called net profit the excess of the flow of profits accruing on a stock of capital over the interest bill involved. It is better to call gross profit the excess of proceeds over outgoings, and net profit the residue after deducting the allowance (however calculated) for amortisation; then interest is regarded as being paid out of net profit. This is a verbal point. A more serious defect is great vagueness about the meaning of the capital value of an operational stock of means of production—equipment and work in progress.

Sraffa set up a simple input–output model of the flow of production, with given employment, and postulated that all inputs used up are replaced in kind in the same period.[12] The net output of the period is then a list of physical quantities of products. The technical specifications do not determine distribution between wages and profits. (This was the main point of the exercise—to lay the basis for a critique of "marginal productivity".) Sraffa takes great trouble to provide a foolproof numeraire in which prices can be expressed, but the Keynesian wage unit serves just as well.

---

[12] See *Production of Commodities by Means of Commodities* 1960.

Now, corresponding to any given rate of profit per period, there is a set of prices at which the output of each commodity pays the wage bill for labour directly and indirectly involved in producing it and profit on the value of inputs that have gone into it. Thus a given rate of profit, in given technical conditions, is consonant with a particular share of net profit, that is the excess of the value of net output over the wage bill, and a particular real-wage rate in terms of any commodity.

In short, to find the rate of profit on capital we must know the technical conditions of production and the share of wages in net output.

Against the background of neoclassical teaching, this may appear startling, but a moment's reflection will show which is the more cogent. The influences which govern the social distribution of income are broadly independent (though there are always cross-connections) of the character of technology. At the present time, commodities of the same engineering specifications are being produced by the same methods in South Korea as in Pittsburg, at a small fraction of the labour cost per unit of output, which makes prospects of profit high in the former and attracts investment and employment away from the latter.

Sraffa makes the dichotomy between technology and distribution absolute by postulating one given self-reproducing specification of production in physical terms, with a given labour force, while leaving the share of wages in net output (which entails the rate of profit) free to be anywhere between zero and unity.

It is not necessary to be confined to Sraffa's discrete periods. The flow of labour time expended, depletion and replacement of stock and the flow of net output are all continuous; the turnover periods of various items determine the relation of the total stock of means of production to the labour force, while wages are paid out in the normal way, week by week.

But how do we close the system, to find the rate of profit and so the value of the stock?

For Pigou, the interest that rentiers demand governs the rate of profit. This concept is unnatural (though Sraffa himself flirted with it). The rate of interest is a short-period, day-to-day phenomenon, depending upon market sentiment, monetary policy and the available stocks of placements in existence at any moment. It influences investment through its relation to the expected level of future profits. (This was the point that Hicks forgot.) Over the long run, the interest that rentiers can exact is dominated by the profits that entrepreneurs can earn, not the other way round.

The classical solution was to take real wages as given in physical terms—as a flow of specified commodities. This was appropriate to the first stages of capitalism, but it is too restrictive for modern times.

For Marx, the key concept was the rate of exploitation (which we may translate as the ratio of net profit to the wage bill) which fluctuates with the balance of forces in the class war. Now we are getting warm, for here is a clue to a theory of distribution. But exploitation determines only the potential surplus yielded by industry. For the surplus to be realised, capitalists must organise employment and turn potential surplus into actual profits.

Finally, to close the system, we introduce effective demand in the form of Kalecki's principle that the workers spend what they get and the capitalists get what they spend. When workers continuously consume their share of net output as wages, the flow of gross profits is equal to the flow of gross investment, plus rentier consumption paid for out of interest and distributed profits. When amortisation allowances are equal to the value of replacements, the flow of net profit per annum is equal to net investment plus rentier consumption. Then long-run normal prices of all inputs and outputs are such as to reconcile the value of the share of profits in the value of net output with a uniform rate of profit on the value of the constituents of the stock of means of production.

Capitalists decide upon gross investment, net investment and distribution to rentiers, but they cannot, collectively, make the rate of profit whatever they please. Workers have a power of veto over the rate of exploitation. When labour is organised, irresistible demands for higher money-wage rates set an "inflation barrier" to an unacceptable share of profits while, even in South Korea, real wages cannot be kept permanently below the level which permits workers to preserve their capacity for toil and to bring up their families.

But now we have burst the bonds of Sraffa's strictly specified model; we must continue the argument in a broader setting.

TECHNICAL CHANGE

Sraffa's model depicts a strictly one-technique economy. The concept of a book of blue-prints of techniques, each installed on an "island" with a different rate of profit, gave rise to a fanciful argument over "re-switching". This cannot be set in historical time, for each island must have had a different past when the stock of means of production appropriate to its technique was built up, and different expectations of the future, appropriate to its rate of profit. Accumulation with a single technique and growing labour force is also a construction in logical time. My "golden age" was intended to depict a single economy growing through historical time with gradually changing technology in which, however, normal long-period prices are continuously realised. The original version was not well specified because of vagueness about the rate of profit. It can now be set out afresh.

The "long period" is not a date in the future when we are all dead. It is a situation in which a given employed labour force is operating a particular stock of means of production to produce a flow of output in such conditions that a uniform rate of profit obtains and will remain constant through time. Such a situation would never be exactly realised at any moment in the history of any actual economy. It is a logical construction, not an hypothesis about the behaviour of capitalist economies. I used it as a base line against which to describe the vicissitudes of a developing economy; I do not know that any better system for combining logical with historical analysis has yet been devised.

In a golden age, new techniques are being continuously introduced in such a way that, as they are installed, the flow of output produced by a given labour force is rising through time at a steady pace. Innovations made at each round are neutral to each other in the sense that they can be implemented without changing the distribution of the labour force between the stages of production. Neutrality in a technical sense does not by itself guarantee a steady rate of growth at a constant rate of profit. For this, further conditions are necessary.

First, the ratio of gross investment to the growing stock of capital must be constant through time. Since the means of production appropriate to the newest best-practice techniques are different from those that are being discarded, net output is not physically distinct from replacements, as in Sraffa's model. We must, therefore, introduce amortisation in a financial sense. In the golden age, amortisation allowances are in a constant proportion to gross investment, and net investment per annum is equal to the growth per annum in the value of capital.

It is also necessary that real-wage rates rise at the same pace as product per man employed, so that the share of wages in net output remains constant, and that the ratio of consumption out of profits to the value of capital remains constant. This ratio may be influenced by the capital gains that accrue to shareholders in successful corporations;[13] therefore to assume a constant ratio of rentier consumption to the value of capital involves assuming that the proportion of investment financed out of retained profits is constant, that the flow of capital gains which this generates is constant, and that the proportion of capital gains realised for expenditure is constant. But it is somewhat anomalous to bring capital gains —an essentially speculative phenomena—into the tranquil conditions of a golden age.

When the requisite conditions are fulfilled, steady growth is maintained with a constant capital to output ratio, a capital to labour ratio rising at the growth rate and a constant rate of profit.

The share of profit affects the level of productivity at any point on the growth path, for it affects the proportions of the labour force operating older and newer techniques. The shortest length of service life of plant, therefore the greatest proportion of the newest, most efficient plants in use, is seen when there is no rentier consumption; that is, when the whole of profits is devoted to investment. The greater the ratio of rentier consumption to the value of the stock of capital, the lower the real-wage rate at any

---

[13] Cf. N. Kaldor, "A Neo-Pasinetti Theorem", *Review of Economic Studies*, October 1966.

point on the growth path and the longer the tail of older, less productive, equipment.

The rate of gross investment and pace of growth of productivity must be in step, but neither one determines the other. High animal spirits and a strong competitive urge to expand causes entrepreneurs to seek out new commodities to produce and new methods of production. At the same time, inventions and discoveries coming from outside private enterprise stimulate investment to take advantage of them.

A necessary condition for steady growth is that real wages rise in step with productivity; when they fail to do so, demand fails to rise sufficiently to absorb potential output, and stagnation sets in.

I first suggested that rising real wages might come about by prices falling with costs. It is more natural to suppose that money-wage rates are rising. But if workers' bargaining power is sufficient to keep money-wage rates rising enough, on average, to offset the average rise in productivity, it is likely to be raising them too much.

There is nothing in the conditions of a golden age to guarantee it against inflation.

As real income rises, both for workers' and rentiers' families, the composition of the flow of output of consumption goods changes. It is treated here merely in terms of the employment and profits to which it gives rise, without any consideration of *utility* or welfare. Tastes come into the argument, but consumers do not know what their tastes are going to be for new commodities until they have seen them. It is the business of producers to decide for what commodities they will be able to create remunerative demand.

The conditions of a golden age can be perfectly fulfilled only if expectations, based on past experience, are turning out to have been correct. This could never be exactly realised. The whole point of the construction is to enable us to classify the conditions that prevent it from being fulfilled.

Short-period conditions concern investment, the ratio of consumption to income, the level of money-wage rates and the availability of finance, all of which can change rapidly from week to week. Long-period conditions concern the structure of the stock of means of production and the distribution of wealth, which change slowly.

The short-period conditions are always present. We are never *in the long period* independently of them. But the long and short-period conditions may be in balance with each other, as in a golden age, or out of balance. For instance, when there has been a shift in technology of the kind which I described as "favourable to capital"—that is, which requires a considerable increase in the capital to labour ratio for the latest best-practice technique—then, if no more than the former level of gross investment is maintained, plants which offer less employment at normal capacity operation are displacing those which offered more. This produces long-period unemployment which cannot be dealt with merely by stimulating effective demand but requires structural changes that do not come about under profit-seeking private enterprise.

I hope that with these elaborations of the formal argument, my old story of the vicissitudes of a developing economy may be more perspicuous.

The essay on the rate of interest, here reprinted once more thirty years after it was written, is quite old-fashioned. It does not deal either with an open system or with inflation, now the topical monetary problems. It only expanded and consolidated the theory as Keynes had left it. However, I hope that it is still useful in providing a defence against modern monetarism, which interprets historical correlations as evidence of causation and is in a chronic state of confusion between flows of income and stocks of wealth.

THE GENERALISATION OF THE
GENERAL THEORY

THE GENERALISATION OF THE
GENERAL THEORY

I. INTRODUCTION

KEYNES' General Theory of Employment is an application to output as a whole of the analysis developed by
Marshall of the short-period equilibrium of a particular
industry. In a typical Marshallian short period, demand
for a commodity (for example, fish[1]) has recently risen
and is expected to remain at its new level. Output is
limited for the time being by the existing capital equipment of the industry (trawlers). Competition prevails and
the price of the commodity is equal to marginal costs to
the firms concerned. Marginal costs are rising sharply
as demand strains against the limits of capacity. Marginal
cost, and therefore price, exceeds average cost, and profits
(quasi-rents) stand at a level which causes the firms
already in the industry to place orders for more capital
equipment, and induces new firms to enter the market.
This corresponds, when extended to output as a whole,
to a situation where prospective profits are inducing a
level of investment which keeps effective demand at a
satisfactorily high level. The reverse case, where demand
has fallen relatively to capacity, is rather lightly sketched
by Marshall. Price is held precariously above average
prime cost by "fear of spoiling the market".[2] Profits are
so low that not only is no new investment going on, but
even existing equipment may not be renewed as it wears
out. The analysis of this situation, extended to output

[1] Marshall, *Principles* [25], p. 369.   [2] *Principles* [25], p. 375.

as a whole, occupies the main part of Keynes' *General Theory*.

To extend Marshall's long-period theory to output as a whole is by no means such a simple matter. In long-period equilibrium the representative firm in an industry is enjoying normal profits, which means that, while some firms may be expanding and others contracting, the industry, on balance, is making no change in its capital equipment. When all industries simultaneously are in this state, there is zero net investment and zero saving for the economy as a whole. This is clearly contrary to the spirit of Marshall's system, which is obviously intended to apply to an expanding economy. But if we take it the other way, and regard long-period equilibrium as some kind of steady expansion, what becomes of normal profits in the representative firm?

There are all sorts of secondary difficulties. The output of an individual firm is no longer limited by a fixed amount of equipment, and firms enjoy "internal economies" as they expand—that is, average costs fall as output grows. What then limits the size of any one firm? Marshall falls back on the argument that, though "there are many fine natures among domestic servants",[1] the sons of successful entrepreneurs are corrupted by life in pampered nurseries, so that before a firm has had time to grow very large, its efficiency decays. But if only one in a thousand picks an able nephew or son-in-law to manage the business in place of his own disappointing offspring, for a generation or two, that firm will end up with a monopoly of the industry.

There are any number of such incidental puzzles. The main difficulty is that, as soon as we envisage an economy in equilibrium with zero net investment, we are plunged into an imaginary world, for the institutions of capitalism,

[1] *Principles* [25], p. 207 note.

4

in actual experience, are closely bound up with the process of accumulation.

Instead of wallowing any longer amongst these contradictions, let us boldly throw away the notion of long-period equilibrium and see how we get on without it.

2. DEFINITIONS AND ASSUMPTIONS

In what follows we shall be concerned with the rate of output of commodities (goods and services) in an expanding economy. The conception of output involves the conception of *utility* in some shape or form, for without it we could not distinguish between a commodity and a heap of dirt. However, we shall not enter into this question but be content to assume that whatever is marketable has utility. We shall be concerned mainly with a movement forward through time, with the stock of capital and the stock of technical knowledge growing as time goes by, so that when we compare two outputs the later one is larger than the earlier, in the sense that there is potentially, if not actually, a larger rate of output of each item of which the earlier output was composed.[1] True, technical progress destroys many commodities, but they are mainly of the non-marketable variety, such as peace and quiet, which do not enter into the calculation of either the smaller or of the larger output.

The "quantity" of output is conceived in the manner made familiar by the conception of the "volume" of exports—that is, outputs are reckoned in their natural units, tons, yards, entertainment-hours, all summed in terms of the prices ruling at some arbitrarily selected

[1] Cf. Samuelson, " The Evaluation of Real National Income " [38], *Oxford Economic Papers*, January 1950.

date (new commodities which have come into existence since the base date being added in at their value in terms of existing commodities).

Capital is conceived in terms of the physical outfit of capital goods required to produce a given rate of production, when working at its designed capacity, with the technique in use.[1] (If we followed Wicksteed in treating consumption as the finishing stage of an industry producing utility[2], we could measure consumption goods in the same way.) We measure all values in terms of the average price of a man-hour of labour, and we ignore the index-number problem which presents itself when wage rates for different types of labour vary relatively to each other. Thus the stock of capital is measured in terms of its cost of production in wage units. Given the relation between money prices and money wages, it can also be reckoned at its value in terms of commodities.

To simplify the argument we will divide the community into three classes, workers, entrepreneurs, and owners of wealth. An entrepreneur normally doubles the role of owner of wealth to some extent, and uses his wealth in his business. Apart from this, he operates with borrowed funds; there is no share capital.

Money and bonds make up the whole supply of paper assets, and there is only one rate of interest—the rate on bonds.

These assumptions are not essential to the argument, but they promote clarity by giving us a definite and simple picture of the economy.

The total of profits is national income, net of depreciation of existing capital, *minus* wages. From the profits they receive entrepreneurs pay over to the owners of wealth

[1] See p. 22.
[2] Wicksteed, *The Co-ordination of the Laws of Distribution* [49], p. 35.

sums governed by the rate of interest which was ruling at the time when they contracted debts to them. The excess of profit over interest is net profit.

The "General Theory" is used in a loose sense, to include Keynes' book and the subsequent development of the ideas contained in it.

3. THE RATE OF INTEREST AS A REGULATOR

Before proceeding with the main argument it is necessary to guard against following a false scent: the conception of an economy which is automatically held on a path of steady development by the mechanism of the rate of interest.

Keynes threw out a suggestion[1], which has been elaborated in various ways[2], that full employment might be maintained by sufficient variations in money-wage rates. When unemployment appears, the argument runs, money wages and prices fall. If the quantity of money is not reduced correspondingly, the existence of cash now redundant to the needs of active circulation causes the rate of interest to fall, and this process continues until the fall in the interest rate has stimulated investment (or reduced thriftiness) sufficiently to restore full employment.

It has been advanced, in support, of this point of view, that while unemployment has been notoriously more prevalent in the twentieth century than in the nineteenth, wages have been notoriously more sticky, and that unemployment can therefore be accounted for by the breakdown of the above mechanism.[3]

---

[1] *General Theory* [21], p. 180.

[2] Pigou, "Real and Money Wage Rates in Relation to Unemployment" [31], *Economic Journal*, September 1937; Hicks, "Mr. Keynes and the Classics" [10], *Econometrica*, April 1937; Modigliani, "Liquidity Preference and the Theory of Interest and Money" [28], *Econometrica*, January 1944.

[3] Pigou, *Lapses from Full Employment* [30], p. 72.

But the analysis raises more problems than it solves and is by no means in a state to bear historical applications.

First of all there is a purely formal difficulty in the way in which the argument is usually stated. It jumps from the total stock of capital appropriate to a certain rate of interest to the rate (say, per annum) at which investment is carried out, so that the rate of investment is represented (given the prospect of profit) as a function of the rate of interest. But clearly we cannot say what rate of investment is appropriate to a given rate of interest without knowing for how long that rate of interest has been ruling and the investment going on.

However, the main point of the argument can be rescued if we say that, at any moment, if the rate of interest falls, the total of investment plans will increase, and the rate of investment is likely to be higher for some time than it would have been if the rate of interest had remained at the former level. On this basis it is, perhaps, legitimate (with due reservations) to speak of a full-employment value of the rate of interest, in a given short-period situation.

But it is by no means easy to see how the monetary mechanism is supposed to ensure that the rate of interest actually assumes its full-employment value. If the economy is conceived to have experienced the operation of this mechanism within living memory it must be supposed that people expect a fall in wages and prices when unemployment threatens to appear. Under the influence of such expectations investment plans are postponed. Thus the appearance of unemployment must be imagined to reduce the full-employment value of the rate of interest by more than it makes the actual rate fall.

On the other hand, if the economy has had no such experience but has lived through prosperous times when the rate of interest had no occasion to fall, the tendency of the rate of interest to respond to changes in the demand for money must have atrophied. Owners of wealth in such a case must be supposed to have been endowed by past experience with a confident belief in a normal value of the rate of interest (that is, a normal price of bonds), and then, if a short-period situation should arise which (according to the theory) required a fall in the rate of interest, the rate of interest would refuse to fall. For as soon as the price of bonds began to be bid up by those who found themselves holding redundant money, plenty of owners of wealth would be willing to sell bonds at the raised price, intending to hold money for a time, and repurchase bonds when their price relapses to normal, thus making a profit on the round trip.[1] Thus the rate of interest could not fall appreciably below its expected value. It could, however, rise above it when the supply of money, relatively to national income, was suddenly reduced, for it is worth while sacrificing interest for the convenience of having money as a medium of exchange. The demand for money, against the rate of interest, at any moment, must then be visualised as somewhat of this form (given national income and the expected long-term rate of interest).

RATE OF INTEREST

QUANTITY OF MONEY

A rise in national income would drive up the rate of interest, but a fall in national income would not lower it; it would merely shift the corner in the curve, at which all money is absorbed in active circulation, back to the left.[2]

[1] See below p. 148. See also Kaldor [15], p. 15. [2] Cf. Modigliani [28], p. 55.

9

Thus, if the system happens to get into a position where the full employment value of the rate of interest lies below its actual value, no automatic corrective is at work. The rate of interest may be assumed to fall after sufficient time has gone by for expectations of its future recovery to be undermined. But meanwhile the rate of investment is low, unemployment is rife, and a slump has set in. By the time the rate of interest comes down, profit expectations have come down still more. The automatic corrective action of the rate of interest is condemned by its very nature to be always too little and too late.

(The above argument is derived from the "liquidity preference" theory of the rate of interest, but it does not depend on uncertainty, indeed it is the very confidence with which the owners of wealth believe in the normal price of bonds that makes the rate of interest so reluctant to fall.[1])

It might still be argued that the automatic reaction of the monetary system can be supplemented by conscious policy, and that sufficiently far-sighted and drastic action could always force the rate of interest to its full-employment value. On this line of thought it might be held that, if anything resembling steady progress has ever been known in reality, it must have been because wise and powerful monetary authorities were controlling the rate of interest in this way. But such a conclusion is untenable for two reasons. Our argument applies to the whole capitalist world, not to one country, but monetary systems are managed nationally, and, until recent times, the overriding objective of monetary policy has been the stability of the foreign exchanges. In some circumstances it may happen that a fall in investment in one country is

[1] Cf. Harrod, *Towards a Dynamic Economics* [8], p. 62. It was Mr. Harrod, I believe, who first pointed out the need to introduce liquidity preference into the " classical " scheme.

accompanied by a strengthening of its exchange rate, making a fall in the interest rate possible, but it would only be by a happy accident which could not be relied upon regularly to occur. A country whose share in world investment mainly takes the form of a surplus of exports, matched by foreign lending, will sometimes find that a spontaneous fall in lending runs ahead of a fall in exports, so that the exchange is strengthened as investment falls, but more often a fall in exports requires a rise in the rate of interest to redress the balance of payments, so that the rate of interest has to be raised just when employment is falling.

The second objection applies equally in an open or a closed system. Monetary control is essentially asymmetrical. It has the power to check an expansion in employment, but it is too feeble to promote one; for while the authorities can always force the rate of interest up at short notice by reducing the quantity of money, the extent to which they can lower it quickly is very limited, even if they are prepared to increase the quantity of money *ad infinitum*.

Therefore mere monetary management cannot preserve full employment. If in reality long periods of expansion have occurred, it must have been because there was some force continually driving the economic system into its bridle. The difference between one period and another lies far less in the behaviour of the monetary mechanism than in the circumstances with which the mechanism has to deal.

4. What is the Bottleneck?

I. FULL EMPLOYMENT AND FULL CAPACITY

Before setting out upon our quest for a long-period theory we must investigate the question of the factors limiting output at any moment.

In the foregoing (as in much current discussion) it was taken for granted that full employment sets the upper limit to the possible rate of output, but this slurs over an important question: the relation between full employment of labour and full-capacity operation of capital equipment.

In the situation depicted in the General Theory, output has fallen below the level attained in the recent past; equipment, as well as labour, is waiting for a revival, and the question of whether full capacity or full employment would be reached first, if a revival occurred, is still remote. In that setting it was natural enough to neglect the distinction between them, but for long-period problems the question cannot be left in such a vague state.

There are a number of possible relations between capacity and available labour:

(1) Capacity may have been abruptly reduced (say, by bombing) relatively to available labour. Men are idle for lack of equipment to work with, although effective demand is high. There is then a strong inducement to invest. But the output of consumption goods has been reduced (by the destruction of equipment and stocks) below what people are accustomed to, and at this low level is highly inelastic. Any increase in the rate of investment therefore leads to a sharp rise in prices, which reduces real wages rates below the level regarded as tolerable even by employers and causes money wage rates to rise, so that we have the spectacle (undreamed of in the General Theory) of the vicious spiral of wages and prices setting in while there is still heavy unemployment.[1]

(2) Capacity may increase abruptly, relatively to available labour. This happens, particularly in "new"

[1] Cf. Hicks, " World Recovery After the War " [13], *Economic Journal,* June 1947.

countries, when a small amount of investment (say, in building a railway, or in prospecting for minerals) brings a large amount of hitherto untouched natural resources into play. Prospects of profit are then high in utilising the new capacity, but hands are lacking, and for a time effective demand strains at the limits of full employment. But available labour meanwhile is rapidly increasing, for immigrants are attracted (not to mention slaves or convicts) so that the supply of labour responds to the demand for it. (Regions as diverse as Malaya and North America were peopled by this process.) At the same time, investment takes the most labour-saving form that existing knowledge permits, and technique is constantly being improved so as to increase output per man-hour. (This seems to be the most likely explanation of the high productivity of labour in American industry.)

There is no reason to expect demand and supply of labour to keep exactly in step, and the new countries may experience an alternation of periods when immigration has overshot the mark, and available labour exceeds capacity, with periods when capacity exceeds available labour.

(3) Capacity may be increasing, not by violent leaps but by a gradual process of accumulation, while population, or rather available labour, is stationary, or increasing at a slower rate. This state of affairs may continue so long as technical progress is raising output per man and so reducing the amount of labour required to operate a given capacity.

(4) Available labour may be increasing faster than capacity. When the size of families is such that available labour, from year to year, increases faster than demand, there is a continuous increase, from year to year, in numbers unemployed. The increasing tendency of population may be kept in check by Malthusian misery, so that every increase in demand for labour increases the supply of

human beings (this was Ricardo's hypothesis). The unemployment may be "disguised" as rural over-population, or it may be continually drained off by emigration to the "new" countries. But, in normal times, in the "old" countries, there is labour available for employment which is not being used.

Thus occasions when available labour falls short of capacity are likely to be rare and an analysis in which capacity is treated as the short-period bottleneck, restricting the possible rate of output at any moment, has more general application than one in which full employment sets the upper limit.

II. FINANCE

There is another kind of check upon the possible rate of accumulation besides capacity and available labour: that is, the supply of finance. A world in which entrepreneurs could borrow without limit at the ruling rate of interest, would be much unlike the world we live in. Unlimited borrowing would be possible only where there was no uncertainty about future profits, not only in the broad, but in respect to the fortunes of individual enterprises. Where there is uncertainty, borrowers must provide lenders with more security than their own hopes, and investment plans are limited by the supply of finance.

Owing to the ambiguous nature of the word *capital* there is a tendency to confuse the supply of finance with the supply of saving.[1] But they must be sharply distinguished, for they operate on totally different planes. A "shortage of capital", in the sense that saving is inadequate, limits the rate of investment which it is physically possible to carry out; it shows itself in an excess of demand for labour over supply, and it is caused by a high proportion

[1] See Robertson, *Essays in Monetary Theory* [32], p. 3.

of consumption to income. A "shortage of capital", in the sense of an inadequate supply of finance, limits the investment plans which entrepreneurs are able to organise. It shows itself in a high risk premium on industrial securities and in difficulty in arranging new loans, and it may be caused by general lack of confidence on the part of owners of wealth, or by the fact that too small a part of total wealth is owned by actual or potential entrepreneurs.

It is true that the amount of finance (including investment of a firm's own funds) actually used during a period is equal to the savings made during the period, because both are equal to the investment made during the period, but there is no direct connection between them. In respect to a particular scheme of investment, the finance which it requires has to be arranged before outlay on investment begins,[1] while the purchase of securities out of the savings which correspond to it are made only after the income which it generates has worked its way through the economy. Nor is the amount of finance available in a particular situation in any way governed by the rate of saving which is going on at that moment. It is perfectly possible for schemes of finance to be arranged on a single day which would keep investment (and saving) running at the maximum possible level for years. On the other hand the existence of idle resources, which indicates that potential saving is running to waste, does nothing to facilitate the supply of finance.[2]

[1] The entrepreneur, to save interest payments, as far as possible avoids borrowing in advance of actual outlay. He prefers to arrange for a " line of credit " (in the simplest case, overdraft facilities at a bank). As the actual outlay on investment is made the credit is used up, the lender providing the borrower with funds by selling out other assets, and accepting his obligations in their place. Thus finance is not normally taken until actual outlay is made, but it must be provided for in advance when the scheme of investment is planned.

[2] Except in so far as the authorities deliberately make credit easy in an attempt to help recovery.

All the same there is an important round-about connection between saving and finance. This is seen most clearly if we go to the opposite extreme from the assumption of unlimited credit and, instead of assuming that every entrepreneur can borrow *ad libitum*, assume that there is no borrowing at all, and that each entrepreneur is confined to investing his own past accumulated savings, so that the only source of funds for investment is "internal finance".[1] Even then, each does not make new investment crumb by crumb as profits accrue. In any one year some are investing and some accumulating reserves by saving out of profits. Each scheme of investment, paid for from reserves, so to speak uses up finance equal to its value. By the time the investment has been completed and expenditure out of incomes earned in making the investment has run its course, savings equal to the value of the investment have been added to wealth somewhere in the economy.

Now, from the point of view of any individual concern, the investment which it will plan to undertake, in any situation, depends upon two things—prospective profits and the amount of reserves at its disposal. Its reserves in turn depend upon the savings which it has made in the more or less recent past. If other members of the community besides entrepreneurs are saving, the addition to reserves of firms made in any period is less than the investment carried out in that period, and the system must soon run down.

But even if all saving were done by entrepreneurs, the system is not guaranteed against trouble, for the distribu-

[1] We must suppose that the entrepreneurs are sufficiently versatile to make investments wherever the prospect of profit is greatest, for, if each invests only in the line of business where he happened to start, production would rapidly get out of step with demand (unless demand in each line happened to expand in just the right proportions) and the prospect of profit in some lines would fall so low that investment in them would cease.

tion of saving between firms may have an influence on the course of investment. Suppose, for instance, that there are some young and enterprising firms, and some old and cautious ones. The young firms commit whatever reserves they may have to investment. A large part of the corresponding savings are made by the old firms. Thus the ownership of uncommitted reserves gradually changes hands. The young firms would like to continue investment, but soon they have no more funds. The old firms have the funds but hesitate to commit them. The rate of investment therefore fails to be maintained, and the system runs down.

Thus not the amount, but the distribution, of saving in one period has an influence upon the course of investment in the next.[1]

We must now remove the assumption that all investment is financed from reserves and introduce rentiers into the picture. The finance to match investment plans is not limited to uncommitted reserves of firms, but can be extended indefinitely by borrowing[2]. The investment plans which can be organised now depend very much upon the distribution of the ownership of wealth. There is

[1] Marx assumes that reserves amassed in one period will always be invested in the next (except in times of crisis). In this case the rate of accumulation is governed by saving, though the mechanism is totally different from that postulated by the monetary theory discussed above.

[2] In the case where each piece of investment is financed by the past savings of the firm which makes it we can speak of the supply of finance in existence at any moment—that is, the sum of uncommitted reserves of firms. When borrowing is possible the supply of potential finance cannot be so definitely conceived. It depends very much upon the credit of would-be borrowers. Moreover, the amount that any one can arrange to borrow, at a particular moment, increases up to a certain point with the interest that he offers, though it does not increase indefinitely, since it is of no use to try to attract finance by offering a rate of interest that no one believes the borrower will be able to honour. (See Kalecki, " The Principle of Increasing Risk ", *Essays in Economic Fluctuations* [16].)

an element of the pawnshop in even the most sophisticated kind of borrowing—existing wealth is pledged as a guarantee for new loans. Thus (given the prospects of profit and the general state of confidence and the reputation of the particular concern) the amount of new borrowing that an entrepreneur can arrange at any moment largely depends upon the ratio of the total debt of the concern to its total assets, that is, on the proportion of its assets that it owns outright. (If the debt of a concern is, say, half the value of its assets, net earnings, reckoned as a percentage on the value of the assets, can fall to half the rate of interest on the debt before the concern defaults or begins to pay interest out of capital.)[1]

Suppose that we start from a position with a given number of entrepreneurs, each of whom owns half the capital which he operates. If each continually makes net saving (in excess of amortisation) at a rate equal to half the investment which he carries out, the ratio of debt to assets remains unchanged (apart from accidental gains and losses) and the supply of finance (so long as prospects and confidence remain constant) will be continually renewed as it is used up.

If more than half of all saving is done outside the concerns, say by rentiers, then the ratio of debts to assets in the concerns is rising, and the power of the original set of entrepreneurs to borrow is gradually exhausted. All the same, investment can continue indefinitely if the class of entrepreneurs is recruited, at an adequate rate, by rentiers using their accumulated wealth to start businesses. (Rentiers may prefer land to industrial securities, so that

[1] See Kalecki [16], p. 99. Mr. Kalecki works out his argument as though new borrowing was governed by the absolute difference between the capital owned by the firm and its "commitments", but he states in a footnote (p. 106) that it is the ratio, not the difference, which is relevant.

there is a tendency for the yield on real property to fall continuously, relatively to the yield on industrial securities, but this tendency is held in check if from time to time a landlord sells his estate and sets up in business, or dissipates his wealth in riotous living, thus swelling the savings of entrepreneurs by the amount of his dissaving.) Alternatively, banks may step in, and borrow from the rentiers—that is, accept deposits from them—in order to take a share in business.

On the other hand, if the net saving of the entrepreneurs that we start with bears a higher ratio to their borrowing than their initial capital to their initial debt (that is, in our example, if their rate of saving is equal to more than half of their rate of investment) the proportion of debt to assets is constantly falling, and the supply of finance to them is growing continually easier.[1] (There may then be a continuous leakage as business fortunes are invested in land, without the supply of finance to industry drying up.)

[1] The ease with which a firm can command finance is not the same thing as its liquidity. When the proportion of its own capital to its total debt is high, the firm is in a favourable position to finance new investment, even if all its capital is already sunk in the business, so that it has no loose funds of its own. Quite apart from this there are the reserves which it has accumulated by saving and which at a particular moment are not yet committed. These provide " internal finance ". A firm will generally be more ready to finance its own investment than outsiders are to finance it. It charges itself, so to speak, a lower risk premium than it would have to pay for outside funds. Thus the existence of a large amount of internal finance promotes investment. This is different again from liquidity in the sense of holding cash. It may happen, over a period when a budget deficit is running, that the savings of firms (together with any borrowing they have made) exceed industrial investment, so that industry as a whole at the end of the period is highly " liquid " in the sense of commanding a large amount of " internal finance ", but it need not be " liquid " in the sense of holding a large cash balance. The motive for holding reserves in cash is fear that the rate of interest may be higher (and the value of securities lower) when the funds come to be used than it is at present. The amount of a firm's cash balance are not an indication of its " liquidity " in the sense of commanding internal finance, but of its liquidity preference in Keynes' sense.

Thus we find once more that the distribution of saving (though not its amount) has in the long run a cumulative influence upon the supply of finance, and so, indirectly, upon the rate of investment.

The price at which finance can be obtained is related to the yield at ruling market prices on securities comparable with those to be issued by way of the new loans; this depends on the total supply of such securities outstanding, in relation to the demand for them, the demand being influenced by the tastes and views of owners of wealth and the supply of other assets, and by the supply of money relatively to the needs of active circulation, in the manner discussed below.[1] A fall in the general level of interest rates tends to lower the price required for new finance (because it reduces the return which the lender can get on his money in other ways) and to increase the amount of finance available on given terms.

Further influences upon the supply of finance may be summed up under two broad headings; first, the state of expectations, and, second legal and institutional arrangements and the habits of lenders. There is a general tendency for the supply of finance to move with the demand for it. It is true, of course, that at any moment there are many excellent ideas which cannot be implemented because those who have conceived them are unable to back them with finance. But, by and large, it seems to be the case that where enterprise leads finance follows. The same impulses within an economy which set enterprise on foot make owners of wealth venturesome, and when a strong impulse to invest is fettered by lack of finance devices are invented to release it (the invention of the joint-stock company with limited liability was a technical revolution comparable to the invention of the

[1] See below, p. 25 *et seq.*

steam-engine), and habits and institutions are developed accordingly (it was possible for the prejudice against banks participating in industry to take root in England, where other sources of finance were forthcoming, but not in Germany, where they were not). On the other hand, in a stagnant economy it is impossible to say whether it is lack of enterprise or lack of finance which prevents development from getting under way.

What is true of the broad sweep of development is also true from year to year in a given economy. A high level of prospective profits and a high degree of confidence in these prospects promote enterprise and at the same time ease the supply of finance.[1] A fall in confidence restricts the supply of finance at the same time as it checks the desire to invest. Thus the supply of finance cannot be regarded as a rigid bottleneck limiting the rate of investment, but must be treated rather as an element in the general atmosphere encouraging or retarding accumulation.

III. LAND

Capital equipment forms a bottleneck only from a short-period point of view. The essence of development is that capital accumulation is going on, so that the bottleneck is constantly growing wider as time goes by. But natural resources are not indefinitely expansible, and land may set a permanent limit to economic growth. Some aspects of this question will be discussed later, but at the first stage of our analysis we will rule it out by postulating an economy which is surrounded by undeveloped territory (with all its endowment of ores, waterways and so forth) of the same economic quality as that already in use, so that, provided that an appropriate part of investment is devoted to transport and the opening up of new

[1] Cf. below, p. 156.

land, there are no long-run bottlenecks caused by limited supplies of vegetables or minerals to impede expansion.

IV. CAPITAL EQUIPMENT

We are left, then, with the capacity of capital equipment as the normal upper limit upon the possible level of output at any moment.

Capacity is a somewhat vague notion. In some productive processes it may have an almost literal meaning—say, the capacity of blast furnaces—but in many the possible rate of output per day or per week from given equipment has no very sharp upper limit. Moreover, the capacity of plant depends upon the length of the working shift, the number of shifts that can be worked per week, and the possibility of overtime.

However, the notion of the limit to the rate of output set by capacity does correspond to practical experience. The entrepreneur in charge of production, at any moment, finds himself either in a "buyer's market" or a "seller's market". In a buyer's market the producer is anxious to get orders "to keep the wheels turning". In a seller's market, buyers are begging him to produce at a faster rate than he can. He responds by raising his prices so as to get the most profit possible in the immediate situation, by filling up his order book and lengthening the delay in delivery, or simply by picking and choosing, meeting the demands of valued customers and refusing the rest (the mixture of these methods chosen varies with the nature of the market and the policy of the individual producer). Meanwhile, if he expects the situation to last, he will set about enlarging his capacity.

The limit to the rate of output in a seller's market may be set by physical capacity in the literal sense, by conventions governing the length of the working day, by marginal costs (including wear and tear of machinery) rising sharply as the rate of output from given plant is pushed above a certain speed, or it may be set by full employment of the existing number of workers with particular skills which require long training.

Where craftsmen are the bottleneck in a profitable market employers may give way to the temptation to poach upon each other's coverts, and attract individual craftsmen by offering them better than the standard wages or conditions of work, but (as Adam Smith observed) each employer is reluctant to start a process of bidding up wages, which can only end by raising costs for all of them without increasing the total supply. Thus it often happens that a limited supply of craftsmen has just the same effect as a limited physical capacity of plant, in raising prices relatively to costs or delaying delivery, when demand expands. Once more, if the situation is expected to last, producers will set about widening the bottleneck by training new men.

All this, though important in reality, is somewhat vague, and to make our analysis neat we may formalise it by assuming that at any moment there is a certain rate of output for each type of commodity (including capital goods) which represents normal capacity working, and that this rate of output can be exceeded, in the short period, only at sharply rising marginal cost. In what follows we shall speak of normal prices and normal profits as those which rule when plant is working at normal capacity.

Further, it is natural to assume that capacity can be divided into two categories, that which caters for the production of consumption goods and that which caters for capital goods. Stocks of consumption goods, of course, form part of capital, so that consumption-goods industries may play a part in investment, and the investment made in a period is not necessarily the same thing as the output of capital goods produced during the period. But there is an important group of specifically capital-goods industries (construction, engineering, the greater part of iron and steel) whose capacity cannot be switched to the production of consumption goods (beyond a very minor extent) though each may produce a fairly wide range of types of capital goods. The following argument is conducted on the assumption that the stock of capital in existence at any moment is divided into an investment and a consumption sector, between which there is only a small amount of overlap.

5. A Developing Economy

I. A MODEL OF STEADY ACCUMULATION

We are now ready to embark upon the analysis of an economy in which accumulation of capital is going on continuously.

We will first examine an ideal case of steady growth, in order to see what conditions are required to make such a state of affairs possible.

At the moment when our story begins there is a certain stock of physical equipment, adapted to the demands which have been ruling for various commodities. This entails that the division of capacity between investment-goods and consumption-goods industries is in the same ratio as the division of gross income between gross saving and consumption. Effective demand is such as to secure full capacity working of the stock of equipment, in both sectors. These conditions give us the total real income of the whole economy. We shall call this by the familiar name of "national" income, though the argument would have to be modified if applied to one nation trading with others. The investment which is going on is in course of enlarging the stock of capital in the expectation of future profits.

How should expectations be treated? If we endow our entrepreneurs with correct foresight, we land ourselves in a hopeless philosophical puzzle about Free Will and Pre-destination. (I foresee that you will read this essay. But suppose you hear that I foresee it, and decide not to out of pique. Then I foresee that you will not. But if I had not been so officious as to foresee it in the first place, you would have read the essay after all.)

There is a simple way out of this difficulty. History has endowed the present not only with a physical stock of capital, but with experience of the past. After a long course of prosperity the entrepreneurs, in our ideal case, know that the present rate of profit has lasted for some time back. They assume that the future will be like the past, and, since in our golden age of steady progress each section of time is like the next, their expectations up till now have regularly been verified. It is these expectations which govern the investment that is being undertaken.

Now we have to consider whether the situation is such that this state of affairs will maintain itself as time goes by.

This is, in essence, the problem that Marx treated by means of the famous "Schema" in volume II of *Capital*, which have recently been revived in modern dress[1]. Marx showed that it is not logically impossible to conceive of steady accumulation taking place indefinitely,[2] but he

---

[1] By Harrod, *Towards a Dynamic Economics* [8], and Domar, "Expansion and Employment" [2], *American Economic Review*, March 1947. See below, p. 30.

[2] Rosa Luxemburg denied this. The reason is that she took seriously Marx's assumption that real wages tend to be constant, while he contradicted it by embodying a constant rate of exploitation in his model. See below, p. 120, and p. 128.

held that "in the crude conditions" of capitalist production it would do so only by an accident.[1] Indeed, as we shall see, the conditions which steady accumulation requires are such as never to be found in reality.[2] All the same, it is useful to set them out, in order to see what their absence entails.

The position that we are looking for cannot correctly be described as "equilibrium" for it has not the property of restoring itself in the face of a chance shock. It is, rather, a position which is free from "internal contradictions" in the sense that it can perpetuate itself continuously provided that no shock ever occurs.

Let us imagine that in our ideal world land and labour are always available as required, that the supply of potential finance is continuously renewed as it is used up, and that the monetary system functions in such a way as to keep the rate of interest constant.

Then the initial position of full capacity working can perpetuate itself provided that the following conditions are fulfilled:

(1) Technical progress goes on at a steady pace, and the age composition of the stock of capital is such as to require renewals at a regular rate. Amortisation allowances are set at the level appropriate to the rate of obsolescence and wear and tear which is being experienced, and, taken as a whole, are being continuously reinvested as they accrue.

(2) The gestation period of capital goods, on the average, is constant, so that there is a regular relationship between investment and the rate at which new capital goods become available for use.

[1] *Capital* [27], volume II, chapter 21, section 1.

[2] Cf. Schelling, "Capital Growth and Equilibrium" [40], *American Economic Review*, December 1947.

(3) Technical progress is neutral on balance, in the sense that the cost in terms of wage units of capital per unit of output falls at the rate at which output per man-hour rises.

(4) Competition between entrepreneurs keeps constant the normal rate of profit, that is, the rate of profit obtainable when effective demand is such as to keep capital working just at capacity.

This, combined with the condition that technical progress is neutral, requires that the real wage per man-hour rises with output per man-hour, and provides that the relative shares of labour and capital in total net income remain constant. In Marx's language, the rate of exploitation and the organic composition of capital both remain constant as accumulation goes on.

(5) The proportion of net income saved remains constant.

The behaviour of the level of prices need not be specified, but the behaviour least likely to disturb the above conditions is found when the average money-wage rate per man-hour rises with average productivity, so that the prices of commodities in general remain constant.

In the initial position we assumed that (steady development having occurred in the past) the stock of productive equipment was divided between consumption and investment industries (including in investment both the construction of capital equipment and the building up of stocks and work-in-progress) in the proportion in which gross income is divided between consumption and gross saving. The investment which was going on was in course of increasing the stock of capital in each sector. The five conditions set out above ensure that this situation is free from any "internal contradictions", that is to say it has no inherent tendency to upset itself. For if the stock of capital continues to increase at the same proportionate rate (reckoned in terms of product) as in the initial position, capacity, output, investment and consumption all increase at that proportionate rate. The stock of capital, as it grows, is continuously worked at capacity; it finds demand for its product growing at the same rate as output and yielding the same rate of profit. The expectations of profit in the light of which investment was planned are continuously fulfilled, and therefore renewed, as time goes by. The initial position continuously reproduces itself upon a gradually expanding scale.

This can be illustrated by a simple numerical example.

Let us suppose that the normal long-run proportion of net national income saved is 10%, that the value of the stock of capital is equal to five years purchase of net income, and that 10% of the stock of capital requires to be reproduced every year. Then 60% of the stock of capital must be devoted to consumption-goods industries, and 40% to investment-goods industries.

The proportion of renewals (10% per annum) is the same in each sector.

Let us suppose that entrepreneurs are choosing to replace capital at the required rate and to increase the stock of capital, measured in terms of product, by 2% per annum cumulatively. The gestation period of capital goods is constant, and we take a "year" to represent a period such that capital created by investment in one year is ready for use in the next.

Then we have the following relations:—

Stock of capital				Annual output				
	Consumption industries	Investment industries	Total	Renewals	Net investment	Consumption	Net income	Gross income
1st year	300	200	500	50	10	90	100	150
2nd year	306	204	510	51	10.2	91.8	102	153
10th year (approx.)	360	240	600	60	12	118	120	180

Thus, if s is the proportion of net income saved ($\frac{1}{10}$ in the example) and T is the period for which net income is equal to the stock of capital (5 years in the example) the steady rate of growth of the stock of capital, and of all other quantities in the calculation, is s per period T ($\frac{1}{10}$ over 5 years, or 2% per annum); or, if we write c for the ratio of the stock of capital to a year's net income (5:1 in the example), the rate of increase per annum is s/c ($\frac{1}{50}$ in the example).

These relations ensure that continuous accumulation is possible, but even when all the necessary conditions for steady progress are fulfilled, its realisation depends upon faith. So long as entrepreneurs expect to find a profitable market for increased output they will maintain investment and so, at one stroke, maintain (expanding) effective demand and provide the equipment to meet it. Once they are smitten with doubt and each waits to see what the others will do, investment becomes insufficient to absorb potential saving and effective demand not only fails to expand but fails to remain at the level which makes the existing stock of capital profitable to operate. Thus the given conditions are not sufficient to ensure continuous accumulation, but they are such as to make continuous accumulation possible.

II. CHARACTERISTICS OF THE MODEL

It must be emphasised that this model of an economy enjoying steady growth does not correspond to the behaviour to be expected from any actual economy. It is nothing more than a piece of simple arithmetic.[1] We shall make use of it in what follows as a standard of reference, in order to classify the various types of disturbances to which actual economies may be subject.

Nor does it represent an ideal objective for policy. As we shall see, steady accumulation may be accompanied by chronic or progressively growing unemployment of labour. This means not only that members of the economy may be suffering disagreeable lives but also that a more rapid rate of expansion is physically possible and could be attained by well conceived and successful economic policy. The rate of increase of income which can be continuously maintained is governed by the rate of accumulation, but there is no reason to suppose that accumulation is in any sense at the most desirable level from the point of view of society.

The distribution of income between labour and capital depends, first, upon the technical conditions which govern the relation of the physical stock of capital to capacity output in the initial position and, secondly, on the rate of profit, that is, the rate of interest *plus* the rate of net profit. If the rate of interest were (and always had been) lower or the entrepreneurs were habituated to a lower rate of net profit, the share of labour and the level of real wages would be so much the higher. There is no reason to suppose that the distribution of income which happens to

[1] Cf. Rosa Luxemburg, *Accumulation of Capital* [23], p. 119.

prevail is either just or expedient, though it must be supposed that a larger share of wages in total income would entail a lower rate of accumulation, both because thriftiness would be less and because the cost of a unit of capacity in terms of product would be greater.

Finally, the rate of technical progress which is being experienced depends upon the advance of knowledge, the enterprise of entrepreneurs, and the prevalence of competition between them, which influences the pace at which new knowledge is put into use. In all these respects the pace and the character of technical progress is susceptible to influence by policy.

Thus our model, while it exhibits the great virtue of continuous smooth development, does not necessarily show a state of affairs which is an optimum in any other respect.

Moreover, the steady path of development in this imaginary golden age does not represent an equilibrium position. Quite the contrary. If for any reason investment were to rise above the steady rate, demand would expand relatively to capacity (in accordance with the multiplier based on the short-period marginal propensity to consume); both capital-goods and consumption-goods entrepreneurs would find themselves in a seller's market, prices would tend to rise relatively to costs, profits would rise above normal; in short, the system would be in a boom. Contrariwise, any fall off in the rate of investment would plunge the economy into a slump, that is, into a position where demand is insufficient to keep the existing stock of capital working at capacity.

In the next section we shall proceed to discuss various influences which may drive an economy into boom or slump conditions, and in the last section we shall discuss the behaviour of an economy after it has fallen into the one or the other. The model of steady development is merely an analytical device to permit us to discuss unsteady development.

6. VICISSITUDES OF A DEVELOPING ECONOMY

I. THRIFTINESS

An important feature in our picture of the golden age of steady progress is that saving represents an unchanging proportion of total income, to which the stock of productive equipment and its distribution between the sectors of industry are appropriate. We must now consider what happens if thriftiness increases (the proportion of income consumed falls), and what influences are likely to make thriftiness alter.

An increase in thriftiness may be induced by an increase in investment plans—in the large, when a society begins to develop habits of enterprise and of thrift together, or in detail, when entrepreneurs limit family expenditure or dividend payments in order to have more funds to plough back into their businesses. Then greater thrift makes possible a greater rate of accumulation. But here we wish to consider the effect of an increase in thriftiness in itself, not induced by some other change in the situation.

(a) Effect of a Rise in Thriftiness

Suppose that the system has been expanding at a steady geometrical rate, in the manner of the golden age, up to a certain moment, and that then thriftiness increases, so that the ratio of consumption to income falls. This means that the increment of demand for consumption goods falls short of the increment of supply made possible by the addition to equipment which took place over the immediate past. Surplus capacity emerges in the consumption-good industries, orders for new capital goods consequently fail to be placed, and the rate of investment falls off (or fails to increase at its former rate). If the change is foreseen before it occurs, investment in the consumption-good industries is curtailed appropriately, and surplus capacity does not appear in them, but this only means that investment falls all the sooner.

If the change came about gradually, instead of in a sudden burst, the effect would be no better. It is true that the system could accommodate itself smoothly to a gradual change if there were some force causing the proportion of investment to income to rise as the proportion of consumption fell off. But an increase in thriftiness, whether sudden or gradual, provides no such force, for it does nothing to induce an increase in investment plans, or (except to the very minor extent that it releases capacity suitable for investment industries) to make possible the speeding up of the rate at which plans are carried out.

It seems, then, that a rise in thriftiness above the level to which the system has become adjusted slows up the rate of capital accumulation.

Here it is necessary to make a short return to the controversy about the rate of interest discussed in the first part of this essay. "Classical economics" is usually represented as denying the above proposition and as showing that an increase in thriftiness is a cause of increased accumulation, the causal links being the behaviour of the rate of interest, and the behaviour of money-wage rates.[1] But "classical economics", in this sense, is a somewhat artificial construction. It is derived by asking questions suggested by the General Theory and then patching together answers from the implicit assumptions, the asides and the *obiter dicta* made, for instance by

[1] An alternative assumption which in some ways seems to fit the "classical" scheme better is discussed below, p. 122.

Marshall, in the course of answering quite different questions. In particular, as was argued above, the supposed classical theory of the rate of interest will not survive being transplanted into the setting of an analysis of historical development. The view that a rising value of money is favourable to accumulation I do not think has ever seriously been maintained, outside the context of pure static theory. Thus so far as "classical economics" is concerned, there does not seem to be any case to answer.

(b) Causes of Changes in Thriftiness

Granted that increasing thriftiness unaccompanied by increasing investment opportunities is inimical to accumulation, the next question to be asked is in what conditions thriftiness is likely to increase.

Keynes, formalising a long tradition of "under-consumptionist" theory, argued that the mere increase of wealth increases thriftiness.[1] This point of view appears at first sight to be supported by the fact that, over the up and down of the trade cycle, consumption increases in a smaller proportion than income (investment bears a higher ratio to income in the boom than in the slump) so that, when national income increases, the increment of saving may be as high as fifty per cent. of the increment of income, while total net saving is only, say, ten per cent. of total income. If this relationship holds good as income per head increases over the long run, the ratio of saving to income must be continuously increasing.

But there is a great deal of difference between an increase in real national income which comes about in the upswing of a boom and an increase due to capital accumulation and technical progress. In a boom, the increase of income goes too fast for consumption habits

[1] *General Theory* [21], p. 219.

34

to be fully adjusted to it,[1] and it is confined to small sectors of the community, whereas the long-run increase in income is gradual and widely diffused. Boom incomes may not be expected to last, so that prudence dictates the building up of reserves.

Moreover, the proportion of profits to national income rises, as a boom develops, above its long-run average, because prices rise relatively to money costs, and the propensity to save which applies to profits is markedly higher than that for wages, or even for rentier incomes. The question can be treated in terms of Marshall's short and long-period supply price: when demand increases, given capital equipment, prices rise relatively to money-wage rates and abnormal profits are earned. When the consequent stimulus to investment has led to an appropriate expansion of capacity, profits fall back to normal. And super-normal thriftiness disappears with super-normal profits.

It is therefore impossible to argue from the high short-run marginal propensity to save to a secular rise in thriftiness.

Nor is there much force in the argument that as real income rises material human wants become progressively more fully satisfied, for wants increase with the power to meet them, especially in a stratified society, where the upper income groups are continually putting ideas into the heads of those below,[2] and where artful salesmanship is continually creating new wants in order to exploit them.

But the "under-consumptionist" case does not rest mainly on the idea that thriftiness must rise with average

[1] Mr. Hicks (*A Contribution to the Theory of the Trade Cycle* [9], p. 31) suggests that the apparent difference between average and marginal propensity to consume is entirely due to time lags, and is no more than a statistical optical illusion.

[2] Cf. Duesenberry [3], *The Theory of Consumer's Behaviour*, chapter III.

income, rather that it must increase with growing in-equality of incomes, and that inequality tends to grow as capitalism develops, because the discovery of ever more ways of substituting power and mechanical devices for human muscle and skill is continuously reducing the share in the product of industry received by labour.

We shall see,[1] however, that *a priori* there is no particular reason to expect technical progress to be "favourable to capital" in the sense that it raises the ratio of capital to output, and statistical investigation, as far as it has gone, suggests that the ratio tends to be fairly constant over the long run.[2]

Moreover, as technique grows more complex it increases the amount of professional and administrative services which industry requires, so that the number of families supported by the non-wage share of total proceeds grows relatively to the number of workers in the narrow sense. Thus even when the share of wages falls, thriftiness does not necessarily increase.

(Technical progress has a further equalising tendency in that it raises the purchasing power of incomes mainly spent upon mass-produced commodities faster than those devoted to personal services and the products of individual craftsmen, but to pursue this point would take us too deeply into index-number problems.)

Another major influence upon distribution is the prevalence of monopoly. Here we must beware of double counting, for, if the degree of monopoly is measured simply by the ratio of gross margins to prime costs, it will appear to rise as a result of a mere increase in the ratio of capital costs to output due to capital-favouring changes

---

[1] See p. 89.
[2] Cf. Stern, " Capital Requirements in Progressive Economies " [46], *Economica*, August 1945.

in technique.[1] Moreover, a prevalent type of quasi-monopoly limits competition in price while allowing it free play in salesmanship of all sorts (a part of which, indeed, may be genuine improvements in the quality of commodities) so that costs, instead of profits, are raised by it. The type of monopoly which is relevant here is that which raises the average rate of profit because it puts obstacles in the way of the process (described below[2]) by which an excess of price over costs is competed away.

It may be that the prospect of enjoying a monopoly, at least for a certain time, is required to induce many innovations, and in so far as this is true, there is an element of monopoly profit in the "necessary supply price" of some commodities.[3] But all the same a growth in the rate of profit due, for instance, to an increase in the minimum investment required by new techniques (which increases risk and reduces the number of entrepreneurs who can command the necessary finance) reduces the share of wages in net output just as much as a rise in profits brought about by nefarious means.[4]

There are reasons apart from the nature of technical change why we should expect monopoly to increase as time goes by. In many industries a few firms, escaping the degeneration described by Marshall,[5] gradually grow and swallow up the smaller fry. And in many an amalgamation or cartel formed in mere self-defence during a period of surplus capacity persists for ever after (though some break down when prosperity returns).

---

[1] Mr. Kalecki ("The Distribution of the National Income", *Essays in Economic Fluctuations* [16]) stated his argument in such a way as to make it appear circular, which has caused its importance to be under-rated.

[2] See p. 80.

[3] See Schumpeter, *Capitalism, Socialism and Democracy* [41], p. 88.

[4] Cf. Keirstead, *The Theory of Economic Change* [18], chapter XI.

[5] See above, p. 4.

But even if there is a tendency for monopoly to increase as time goes by, there is a powerful counter-acting force in the development of Trade Unions, which persuade the monopolists to pass back a part of their profits to the workers, in the form of wages and amenities, in order to avoid industrial strife.

From all this it appears that, although there is much to support the under-consumptionist view that the share of wages in income must fall as capital accumulates, and thriftiness increase, yet it is also possible that the counteracting forces may be sufficiently powerful to reverse the result.

II. THE SUPPLY OF LABOUR

The conditions which make the golden age of steady accumulation possible entail that total output increases at the same proportional rate as the stock of capital measured in terms of product. The demand for labour is increasing or shrinking according as the rise in output per man-hour, due to technical progress, goes on at a slower or a faster pace than the increase in total output. When output per man-hour rises faster than total output there is a continually growing amount of technological unemployment, or a continual fall in hours worked per man-year. When output per man-hour is rising more slowly, the demand for labour is increasing.

We must now consider the inter-action between the demand for labour and the growth of population.

There are many complicated and important questions connected with the age, class and sex composition of a population which are bound up with changes in its rate of growth, and with the length of past time that any given pattern of growth has been experienced. All this group of problems we shall ignore, setting out only a crude argument in terms of absolute numbers of "men".

The two aspects of the problem which are most germane to our argument are (a) the cessation of population growth after it has been going on for some time and (b) the continuance of population growth at an excessive rate.

(a) Cessation of Growth in Numbers

First consider an economy which has been enjoying steady progress, in the manner of the golden age, in which technical progress is raising output per man-hour less fast than capital is accumulating. This has been possible because population has been growing, and every year more hands are producing and more mouths consuming than the year before.

Let us suppose that, by a fortunate accident, accumulation of capital and growth of population are in harmony so that the rate of growth in the numbers of workers required to operate the ever-growing stock of capital at normal capacity is just about equal to the rate of growth in the number of available workers. So long as slumps are avoided, unemployment is a small and fairly steady proportion of the ever-growing total of employment.

Since the growth of real income per head is insufficient to keep demand expanding at the same rate as capacity output, the system, so to say, relies upon the increase in population to keep it running. What would happen if the growth of population slowed down?

As soon as entrepreneurs, each in his own line, foresee that the market for commodities will cease to expand at its former rate, they curtail investment plans, a slump sets in and profits fall below normal. If they fail to observe what is happening and go blindly on with investment plans at the rate appropriate to the former situation, excess capacity emerges and consequently the slump, by being delayed, is so much the worse when it comes.

This decline in investment would be offset if there were a corresponding decline in propensity to save. The change in the pattern of life entailed by a change in the rate of growth of population must certainly affect every aspect of the economy, but there is no presumption that any change in thriftiness which results from it will be sufficient to offset the decline in investment; or even that it will be in the right direction.[1]

Assuming that (in the absence of conscious interference with the *laisser faire* economy) the propensity to consume is no greater than it was when population was increasing faster, the economy has fallen into a slump. The community, now, is suffering from "underconsumption" in the purest sense. It has a propensity to save appropriate to a higher rate of accumulation than now appears profitable to its entrepreneurs.

Though the trouble is due to failure of its numbers to increase, it is in no sense suffering from a "scarcity of labour", for, quite apart from the unemployment caused by the slump conditions, there is redundant labour in the investment industries. If consumption were to increase above its former level, there would be labour available to meet demand. Lack of mobility, it is true, may be an impediment to transfers of labour from one sector to another, but the question of mobility fails to arise, for in fact, far from increasing, total consumption falls as a result of the fall in incomes derived from investment activity, and there is general unemployment of the all-too familiar kind.

(Though this situation can properly be described as "underconsumption" it does not follow that, if the community were to depart from pure *laisser faire* and try

[1] Cf. *Papers of the Royal Commission on Population, Report of Economics Committee* [4], p. 45.

to deal with the position by a conscious policy, an increase in consumption would be the best policy to adopt—that is quite another story.)

(b) Over-population

Now consider a case with steady accumulation and neutral progress as before, but with the population growing at a faster rate than the demand for labour. Let us assume first of all that there are no opportunities for employment except those offered by capitalist enterprise, and let us compare the position at two points of time divided by an interval during which the population has increased.

Does the existence of available labour tend to increase the amount of employment? Clearly it increases human needs, but does it increase effective demand?

In so far as State or individual charity provides consumption for the unemployed at the expense of saving that would otherwise be made—that is, in so far as consumption of the recipient of charity is additional to and not in substitution for the consumption of the givers (or tax payers)—the level of consumption (at a given level of investment) has been raised and consequently the total level of employment in consumption industries is greater. But this cannot have eliminated unemployment, for if it did it would not. As soon as the unemployed were off their conscience the rest of the community would return to a higher rate of saving. It requires a growing amount of unemployment to keep employment increasing in this way.

Moreover, the contribution which "doles" make to the consumption of the unemployed may be very small. "It's the poor what helps the poor", and most of what the unemployed consume is not additional demand. If the unemployed are supported by friends and relations who in any case have no margin for saving, an addition to the number of mouths to be fed has no effect upon total consumption, and therefore no effect upon output and employment at all.[1]

(It may seem unduly pessimistic to argue that both an excess and a deficiency in population growth causes unemployment, but we should look at employment, rather than unemployment, to see what is happening. In the first case, a fall in the rate of growth of numbers causes a fall in the rate of growth of employment; in the second case employment increases at its former rate, but it increases by less than available labour, so that unemployment increases also.)

The existence of the " reserve army " of unemployed workers reacts upon employment in another way. It weakens the bargaining position of labour and makes it impossible for Trade Unions to keep monopoly profits in check. Thus prices tend to be higher relatively to money-wage rates than they are where full employment and full capacity coincide. In consequence, the competitive advantage to be gained by finding labour-saving techniques is weakened. Moreover, since the price of equipment (as of other commodities) is raised relatively to wage rates by the high rate of profit, capital-saving techniques are likely to be sought for even if they are actually labour-using. Consequently employment per unit of output is kept high. This is the reverse of technological unemployment.[2] Thus compared to an economy which has

---

[1] Cf. Kalecki, *Studies in Economic Dynamics* [17], p. 88 note.

[2] Static equilibrium with full employment requires that the rate of interest should be such as to induce techniques to be used that will employ all available labour. There does not seem to be any place for this argument in the above analysis, since there is no reason why the existence of redundant population should raise the rate of interest so as to make a given amount of capital employ more labour. It often happens, however, that

developed without redundant labour, an economy with a large reserve army of unemployed workers may have a reserve of productive capacity, which more capital would release, also within the labour force which it does employ.

There is another channel through which some of the redundant workers may get themselves into employment, and that is through the demand for housing. A growth in the numbers supported by a given family income deflects demand from consumption goods in general to demand for housing (a man would rather wear clogs in his own house than leather boots in his mother-in-law's). We shall not consider a country where the unemployed can build themselves hovels of mud, but one where housing is provided by capitalist enterprise. Now, the industry whose output is room-years of living space employs exceptionally little current wage-labour, so that more of the flow of expenditure on house-rent goes to capital than is the case with almost any other kind of outlay. Thus a deflection of demand from things in general to housing has the same effect as a bout of innovations "favourable to capital" and tends to promote investment in the same way. (This cannot, of course, provide a permanent cure for unemployment due to an excessive rate of growth of population, for it requires a given rate of growth to maintain given employment in building.) The effect of an increase in house building is powerfully reinforced if the society concerned has certain standards of public health so that, if not housing itself, at least the auxiliary services of drainage, etc. are provided at public expense.

Thus it is an exaggeration to say that the existence of

a scarcity of finance and a surplus of labour are found together, for both are features of "under-developed economies". Limited finance and a high rate of interest reinforce the tendencies above described to keep output per man low and therefore employment per unit of output high.

available labour has no influence at all on the amount of employment.

The assumption that all employment is given by capitalist enterprise is also exaggerated. No society is so completely specialised as to make self-employment quite impossible. The reserve army can usually produce some kind of output, for its own use or for trade with the capitalist sector. Industries may be built upon material salvaged from capitalist rubbish heaps (petrol tins in Syria). Personal services are pressed upon whoever has a copper to spare (shoe-blacks in Spain) and layers of middlemen squeeze themselves into every gap between cost and demand-price (traders in Africa)[1].

The distinction between employment and "disguised unemployment" in a slump, though not absolutely clear cut, is a straightforward conception. Workers have been expelled from jobs that they were recently holding, and will return as soon as they are sent for. In a developing economy the line is not so easy to draw, for the self-supporting members of the reserve army are tiny capitalists (even a couple of old petrol tins is a stock of capital goods if they are in process of being made into saucepans), and may even employ each other for wages. The "kulaks" among them approximate to capitalist employers. However, the distinguishing characteristic of their industry is that it has a very marked inferiority in productive efficiency to regular employment, and that their propensity to consume is markedly higher than that of regular capitalists, because they are living very near the minimum of subsistence.[2]

[1] Cf. Bauer and Yamey, " Economic Progress and Occupational Distribution ", *Economic Journal*, [1] December 1951.

[2] The several types of unemployment cannot be exactly distinguished, but schematically we may divide them as follows: Write A for the total of labour available, E for the actual level of employment and N for the

The whole picture is radically different when there is land available to be taken into cultivation outside the capitalist sphere. Where the workers who are not offered employment by capitalists can set off into hitherto unpeopled territory where they can support their families by their own labour, their departure relieves the situation in three ways: first, they find themselves a less wretched means of life; second, by removing the enervating influence of redundant labour, they stimulate the capitalists at home to improve technique; and third, their trade, in due course, with the centres they have left, causes the total of effective demand to expand at a faster rate, and so sets up an inducement to invest in capitalist industries which export to them.[1]

(The safety valve of migration to the New World from areas of surplus population was an essential part of the mechanism of nineteenth-century capitalism, and now that it is choked up we begin to realise how much it contributed to the working of the machine.)

III. THE SUPPLY OF LAND

In our model of the golden age there is free land available to be taken into use as required; we must now consider the case, familiar in economic theory, of a capitalist

---

amount of employment required to work the existing stock of capital at its normal capacity. Each is a number of man-hours per year. Each category is rough at the edges and must be thought of as a band of values rather than a single number.

Now, $A - E$ is the total of unemployment;

$\quad A - N$ is the reserve army of labour;

$\quad N - E$ is unemployment due to a slump.

The excess of the value of N at one technique over its value for the same rate of output after labour-saving innovations have been made is potential technological unemployment, which may be absorbed by reducing work per man year.

[1] See below p. 127.

economy which already occupies all the space there is, that is, with a fixed supply of land.

From a formal point of view land may be regarded as a special kind of capital equipment the supply of which cannot be increased, but can be permanently maintained with a small upkeep cost (we shall not enter into the special problems of mining—that is, using up of natural resources). To introduce scarce land into our analysis we will divide output into two categories: agricultural commodities, which we shall call "wheat", and "manufactures", which require a neligible amount of land.

In order to reduce the problem to its bare essentials we will at first make the following extreme assumptions.

(1) The demand of an individual consumer for wheat does not increase with his income.

(2) Substitution between wheat and manufactures is negligible, so that the demand of an individual for wheat is highly inelastic to its price in terms of other commodities.

(3) All land is alike.

And throughout the argument we will assume that:—

(4) Innovations are neutral as between labour and capital so that capital per unit of labour does not vary.

(5) The rate of profit is constant.

First we will examine the case where the yield of wheat per acre is rigidly fixed by natural conditions, whatever technique of production is used.

Technical progress is going on, both in industry and in agriculture, which raises output per man-hour, and so reduces the labour required to produce a given output equally of wheat and of manufactures.

We will first consider a case where the population is stationary, and where industry happens to be expanding just fast enough to absorb its own technological unemployment and to take on the workers released from agriculture by labour-saving innovations in the production of wheat. The total of man-hours per year being worked in the economy as a whole is then constant. The output of wheat is constant and the output of manufactures is rising as time goes by.

Now examine the economy at two points of time divided by an interval in which technical progress has taken place. The cost of wheat, reckoned in wage-units, has fallen, but demand for wheat is unchanged and so is the amount available. The price of wheat, relatively to wages, is constant, while the prices of manufactures have fallen with their costs. The real wage per man is constant in terms of wheat, and has risen in terms of manufactures. The whole of the fall in cost of production of wheat has accrued to land owners as an increase in rent. The terms of trade between industry and agriculture have turned in favour of agriculture.

Now, still with full employment, imagine that the population has increased. The demand for wheat has risen with the number of mouths. The price of wheat has risen, relatively to wages, to whatever extent is necessary to cut back demand to equality with the fixed supply (however inelastic an individual's demand may be, his consumption must suffer a reduction at some point as his real purchasing power falls). Rent per acre has been increased (in terms of wage units) by the rise in the price of wheat as well as by the fall in the cost of an acre's output of wheat. The real wage in terms of wheat has fallen. (If wheat consumption was formerly at subsistence level, Malthusian checks have prevented the increase in population from being realised, and the wage rate has not fallen for those who survive.)

Next suppose that population has increased but employment has not. There is no dole and employed workers are supporting their unemployed relations. The total demand for wheat has increased by less than in the former case, and in the limit has not increased at all. Then the wage rate in terms of wheat is unchanged, but the consumption of wheat per head has fallen (more mouths are fed from each unit of wages).

Now, returning to the case where population and employment have remained unchanged, let us remove the assumption that the yield of land is fixed and suppose that land-saving innovations have been made (say, an improved breed of wheat has been introduced) so that the yield of wheat per acre has gone up. Since the quantity demanded is unchanged, the price has fallen abruptly to equality with cost of production (including profit on the capital employed in agriculture) and rent has disappeared at a stroke. From now on, the real wage in wheat will rise *pari passu* with the real wage in terms of manufactures as labour-saving progress continues in each.

These examples illustrate the generalisation that movements in the real wage rate in terms of wheat depends mainly upon the relation of the growth of numbers employed to the rate at which land-saving innovations are made, and that the terms of trade between wheat and manufactures depends upon the inter-action between the above relation on the one hand and the rate of technical progress in manufactures on the other.

Any number of complications can be woven around this simple analysis. It was unnatural to assume that the demand for land does not increase with real income. The demand for food is not absolutely inelastic, even at a very high standard of life, and land provides many consumer goods (gardens, golf courses) for which demand rises with income. Thus, even in the first case, with constant population, we should allow for some rise in the price of wheat (which stands for all the produce of land) as real income in terms of manufactures rises. On the other hand, if output per acre were not rigid but could be increased, though at diminishing returns, by using more labour and capital per acre, the rise in price of wheat when total demand increases is mitigated. Again, where land is not all alike, a bout of land-saving innovations (with a given total demand for wheat) does not eliminate rent altogether, but throws some land out of cultivation and leaves some Ricardian rent to the rest.

This is all well-trodden ground, and we need not pause to examine it further, but there is another aspect of the matter which is of importance for the present argument: that is the influence upon demand for manufactures of changes in the amount of rent. As the price of wheat in terms of manufactures rises the purchasing power over manufactures of rent income is raised at the expense of wage incomes and capitalist incomes alike. If the owners of land are similar in their spending habits to other owners of property, this increases the thriftiness of the economy as a whole. There is no offsetting increase in the inducement to invest, for demand for manufactures fails to expand in proportion to the former rate of expansion of output and the former rate of accumulation cannot be profitably maintained. In such a case the limitation upon the supply of land would be a continuous drag upon effective demand, which might end by bringing expansion to a standstill.

But this picture is not very life-like, for land is not just the same as other kinds of property. The recipients of rent may be of various social types. Old-style landlords are notoriously a spending class, and so are tycoons who retire to the country to dissipate fortunes derived from industry in amateur farming. What if the land is owned by peasant farmers? They are usually credited with an exceptionally low marginal propensity to consume,[1] but this opinion is based upon the fact that, from year to year, their expenditure is found to be more stable than their incomes (debt incurred in bad seasons being partly paid off in good seasons). A permanent increase in income (good years averaged with bad) such as occurs in the case we are examining, may be presumed to lead to a permanent increase in their rate of consumption of industrial products, including in consumption saving in kind (or investment financed out of income, whichever we like to call it) as they build up equipment on their farms.[2]

Where the recipients of rent spend all they get, our former argument is reversed, for that part of the rise in rent which is at the expense of profit is partly at the expense of saving by capitalists, so that total outlay on the industrial sector is increased by the transfer from profit to rent, and the improving terms of trade of agriculture give buoyancy to effective demand (though, of course, where total population is increasing, the falling real-wage

[1] Duesenberry [3], p. 62.

[2] Where the peasants' savings go into an ever-growing hoard of gold, we have to inquire what would have happened to the rate of gold mining, and what would have happened to the annual increment in the stock of gold above ground, if the peasants had not absorbed it. In so far as the peasants acquire gold that is already above ground, or would have been mined in any case, the effect upon the industrial sector is a leakage of demand equivalent to an import surplus matched by export of capital assets, complicated, perhaps, by monetary troubles; but if the peasants acquire gold which would not have been mined if they had not been ready to take it, the effect is just the same as if they spent their incomes upon any other kind of output.

rate in terms of wheat is an extremely serious matter for the industrial workers).

In this case (which seems likely to be the most common) land-saving innovations, which reduce the price of wheat in terms of manufactures and increases the real purchasing power of industrial incomes, lead to an increase in demand in the industrial sector for its own products which is less than the fall in demand coming from the agricultural sector, so that a slump is precipitated in industry. Thus, so far as effective demand is concerned, plenty rather than scarcity of land appears to be a menace to capitalist prosperity.[1]

An economy which in the past has enjoyed free land and has been expanding in space must undergo many radical changes when it reaches the limit of available land, and rent begins to emerge, but there does not seem to be any reason to expect it to fall into a chronic slump.

The case is very different when free land was used to be taken up ahead of the expanding circle of capitalist enterprise by redundant labour from industry. Then the "closing of the frontier" reacts upon the capitalist sector by cutting off a source of expanding demand on which it has grown to depend, as well as by increasing the misery of the workers and, perhaps, weakening the stimulus to technical progress, in the converse of the manner described above.

There is another way in which the supply of land may have an extremely important influence upon capitalist development. Consider an economy in which land has been scarce for some time, the terms of trade tilting in favour of agriculture and rents rising. Now a new territory is discovered, or some large-scale innovation in

[1] The contrary opinion of Ricardo depends upon assumptions which rule out the possibility of a deficiency of demand.

transport brings a territory formerly inaccessible to capitalism over the horizon of possible exploitation. The effect upon the rents of land already in use is similar to that of a sudden burst of land-saving innovations, and the consequent adverse effect upon the incomes of the "old" agriculturists may, as we have seen, have a tendency to reduce the propensity of the economy to consume. But the effect is likely to be swamped for a long time, perhaps for generations, by the increase in inducement to invest represented by opportunities for profit in opening up the new lands. The glacial pace of accumulation that we have imagined in our model of an economy enjoying steady progress is then suddenly turned to a rushing torrent. An economy which has enjoyed this stimulus from time to time in the past, and then finds itself in a present in which there are no more worlds to conquer, suffers a profound shock. (This is perhaps the best place to look for a clue to the characteristic difference between nineteenth and twentieth-century capitalism.)

IV. THE SUPPLY OF FINANCE

One of the prerequisites of continuous expansion is that the supply of finance (that is, the purchasing power at the disposal of entrepreneurs, whether from their own wealth or their capacity to borrow) should be renewed at an adequate rate as it is used up in schemes of investment. The inflow into the pool of potential finance may fall short of the actual outflow for a number of reasons which have already been discussed,[1] and need only be re-capitulated here.

(a) *Money.* Out of every increment of privately owned wealth, made by accumulating savings, a part will

[1] See above, pp. 14 et seq.

normally be held in the form of money. Moreover a continual growth of national income in money terms requires a growing total of money in active circulation. If the supply of money fails to increase correspondingly, the increment of demand for other paper assets falls short of the increment of supply which corresponds to an increment in stock of real capital, and so there is a tendency for the rate of interest to rise and new borrowing to become difficult.

(b) *Land.* A similar effect is seen where each increment of private wealth increases the demand for "real property" the supply of which is fixed. The yield on land (rent over purchase price) then falls continuously relatively to the yield on industrial assets, and the cost of new borrowing for industry tends to be raised.

(c) *Distribution of reserves.* Where it happens that the most successful firms are the most cautious, and they follow the policy of the dog in the manger, failing either to carry out schemes of investment themselves or to lend to their more venturesome colleagues, the pool of finance is continually being syphoned off into reserves which are held in cash or gilt-edged assets, and the rate of interest or the risk premium on new borrowing is gradually pushed up.

(d) *Confidence.* The consequences of a collapse of financial confidence (refusal to lend) are too well known to need elaboration.

The first three causes may set a gradually increasing drag on accumulation. The last jerks it sharply to a halt, usually after some other cause has undermined confidence in the expectation of future profits.

The converse of all these causes eases finance and assists the maintenance of accumulation.

Innovations in the supply of finance (such as the application of the hire-purchase system to house building) may suddenly make it possible to satisfy a formerly latent demand for investment, and bring about a spurt of accumulation.

V. THE RATE OF INTEREST

We must also consider the direct effects of changes in the rate of interest. When the process of adjustment to a fall in the rate of interest involves a change over to more capital-using techniques for the rate of output already being produced, and transfers demand to more capital-using types of consumption (as when a fall in house rents increases outlay on living space from a given family income), then, as we shall see,[1] it may require investment not offset by a corresponding increase in saving by entre-preneurs. Something of this kind is likely to occur even if techniques are physically unchanged and markets so imperfect that prices are very sticky. A fall in the rate of interest raises the capital value of assets expected to yield a given return (the number of years' purchase of its rent at which a standing house will sell is raised) and this encourages investment in them up to the point at which a fall in average utilisation restores their price once more to equality with their cost of production (the stock of houses to meet a given demand is increased until the interval between lettings reduces average rent received to equality with the rate of interest on the capital cost of a new house). Thus a fall in the rate of interest gives rise to a once-and-for-all burst of extra investment.

It may lead to a once-and-for-all burst of extra consumption as owners of wealth, who find the real purchasing power of their stock of property increased, reduce it

[1] See p. 98.

towards its former level by dissaving—"spending out of capital". It may also give a permanent downward jerk to thriftiness (though here, as Mr. Harrod has failed to disprove,[1] the reaction may be in the opposite direction). Thus a fall in the rate of interest may precipitate boom conditions, and a rise, slump conditions.

A fall in the rate of interest expected in the near future checks investment. An expected rise in bond prices tempts entrepreneurs to use their available funds in the bull market (or in lending at a high short rate to bulls) instead of in schemes of real investment, which they consequently postpone. Thus a rise in the rate of interest which is expected to be reversed is a greater deterrent to investment than one which is regarded as permanent.

VI. OTHER VICISSITUDES

Some other disturbing influences may be mentioned briefly, as they are well known and obvious in their effects.

(*a*) *Prices*.

A rise in the general level of prices such as occurs when money-wage rates shoot ahead of rising productivity, reduces the purchasing power of rentier incomes.

The characteristic of rentier incomes is that they are fixed, by long-term contracts, in money terms. The batch of new contracts entered into today are made in the light of today's prices, but the bulk of rentier incomes being received at any moment are based on contracts made at some time in the past. The main contracts, apart from private house-rents, are entered into by entrepreneurs (debenture interest, managerial salaries) so that the advantage of a fall in their real value mainly accrues to

---

[1] See Graaff, " Mr. Harrod on Hump Saving " [6], *Economica*, February 1950.

net profit, the category of incomes with the highest marginal propensity to save;[1] thus a fall in the real income of rentiers tends to reduce consumption. At the same time, and for the same reason, the burden of debt upon entrepreneurs is reduced and the supply of finance eased. On the other hand, the "money-illusion" of accountants, and legal requirements, which lead entrepreneurs to keep the value of their capital intact in money instead of in real terms, tend to reduce thriftiness.

An expectation of rising costs in the future stimulates investment, for capital goods created now will live into a future when their value is expected to be higher. An expectation of rising prices, moreover, causes ordinary consumers to take on something of the character of entrepreneurs and to "invest" in stocks of durable goods. A sharp and immediate expectation of a rise in prices precipitates hyper-inflation and endangers the stability of the economy, but a vague general impression that prices in the future are more likely to rise than to fall gives buoyancy to effective demand.

A fall of prices, such as occurs as a result of increasing productivity with constant money-wage rates and a constant rate of profit, compared to a constant price level (money wage rates rising with productivity) increases the share of rentier income at the expense of profit, and so is relatively favourable to consumption and unfavourable to the supply of finance, but in this case the "money illusion" tends to increase thriftiness.[2]

A fall in money wage rates accentuates these influences, and, if too rapid, may disrupt the economy by causing a financial crisis.[3]

---

[1] Kalecki [16], p. 87.   [2] Cf. Harrod [8], p. 30.

[3] Cf. Keynes, "Consequences to the Banks of the Collapse of Money Values", *Essays in Persuasion* [20].

An expectation of a future fall in money-wage rates restricts consumption and investment and sets a drag upon accumulation, the converse of the effect of an expectation of rising wages.

(b) *Changes in Tastes.*

Changes in the objects of consumption, if gradual, need produce no disturbing effects (provided that they are neutral between capital and labour) for productive capacity can be switched from one line to another by changing its character as it is renewed in the normal course out of amortisation funds, and the supply of skilled labour can be adapted to requirements (though this may be a more troublesome process) by normal wastage and recruitment. But a sudden and large switch of demand from one commodity to another causes super-profits, a speeding up of investment, and possibly a rise in relative wage rates, in the expanded market, and losses, disinvestment and unemployment in the contracted market. Since investment is concentrated over a shorter time than disinvestment, a sufficiently great swing in demand may cause a boom,[1] while later total investment is at a lower level than it would otherwise have been until the redundant capital in the shrunken market has been worked out of existence.

A change in demand in the direction of simplicity of tastes and home-produced pleasures causes a general slump (as in Mandeville's bee-hive).

(c) *Changes in Technique.*

The most important source of disturbances in an expanding economy lies in the very process of technical change which is the mainspring of expansion. An un-

[1] Cf. [35], p. 38.

foreseen slowing down in the stream of innovations, as we shall see,[1] tends to cause slump conditions, and a speeding up tends to cause a boom, particularly when it takes the form of a sudden, important invention which causes a great bout of innovations to be made.

7. FOSSILS

Since a private-enterprise economy is subject to so many vicissitudes, it can never in fact enjoy steady progress, and we must abandon the artificial device of imagining it to confront each change of fortune with a history of smooth development behind it.

One of the basic assumptions of our model of steady progress was that the age composition of the stock of capital was such as to require a constant proportion of renewals every year. Where over the past (going back perhaps fifty years and more) there has been an alternation of periods of rapid and sluggish investment the stock of capital carries within itself fossils of its own past (just as the profile of a population table betrays the past history of the birth rate). Then renewals, instead of falling due in a regular stream, come in sudden rushes, divided by periods when the accumulation of amortisation funds exceeds current expenditure on replacement, and "echoes" of the original speeding up or retardation of the rate of investment repeat themselves several times before dying out.[2]

Another arbitrary assumption that we made was that the gestation period of capital equipment does not vary from year to year, so that the capital that has newly

---

[1] See p. 104.

[2] Cf. Marx, *Capital*, volume II [27], chapter 20, section ii, and Robertson, *A Study of Industrial Fluctuation* [33], p. 37.

become available for use at a certain moment is equal to the investment carried out over a constant length of past time. Where the gestation period telescopes in and out with changes in the physical nature of capital goods, the rate of change of the stock of capital may vary sharply from one year to another even when it is developing steadily from lustrum to lustrum, and this may set up disturbing reactions on investment and income.

The fossils embedded in the stock of capital (and in the supply of labour trained to various occupations or settled in various districts) destroy the possibility of perfectly smooth development, though a strongly running stream of accumulation may sweep over them without noticeable checks.

The most important consequence of a troubled past lies in its influence on expectations. Experience of prosperity in the past creates conditions favourable to prosperity in the present, and fear breeds the disasters which it fears. The key assumption in our story of a golden age of expansion was confident belief in future profits at a steady level.

But in fact entrepreneurs are looking back over a disturbed past which teaches them that anything may happen in the future. This is even more true for any one line of industry than it is for the system as a whole. Entrepreneurs do not (and have no business to) think globally. Each is interested in a narrow range of markets. And each section of the economy has all sorts of vicissitudes even when the whole is developing fairly steadily. Thus it is not rational to expect a steady future, and, what cuts much deeper, it is not rational to expect anything in particular with great assurance, for experience teaches that expectations generally turn out to be mistaken. This enormously enhances the weight which is given to the present, for it is all that there is to go by, and one must go by something.[1]

In each of the vicissitudes listed above we broke off the story at the point where a boom or a slump began. This was because it would have been idle to go on with the tale while we were still making use of the assumption of given expectations. In fact, a boom changes expectations favourably, and a slump unfavourably, so that each source of disturbance amplifies itself.

8. INSTABILITY

I. THE END OF A BOOM

We have now emerged from the mythical golden age of steady progress into unstable times. (And, by the same token, we have come into a territory well ploughed up with theories, though as yet little harvested of certainties.)

When the rate of investment rises relatively to what it has been in the recent past, consumption increases, in accordance with the short-period marginal propensity to consume,[2] and there is a secondary wave of investment in working capital, and a further increase in consumption. Now in some lines producers find themselves in a seller's market (demand exceeding capacity) and the optimists among them (or those with strong animal spirits[3]), acting on the assumption that the demand will last, place orders for equipment to enlarge their capacity. So the upswing in investment amplifies itself.[4]

---

[1] *General Theory* [21], p. 149.

[2] There has been a great deal of study of the time lag in this movement. See Hicks, *A Contribution to the Theory of the Trade Cycle* [9], chapter II.

[3] *General Theory* [21], p. 162.

[4] The alternative formulation in terms of the " accelerator " is discussed below, pp. 131 *et seq.*

At some point the rise in the rate of investment reaches a limit (we shall return to this point in a moment) and income reaches a maximum. Meanwhile new plants have begun to emerge from gestation; soon there is more capacity to cater for a rate of outlay that has ceased to rise. The sellers' market disappears (at best capacity only just catches up with demand—more often it over-shoots the mark). The rate of investment therefore falls off, income declines, and the boom collapses.[1]

So much is familiar, and (apart from fine details) generally accepted. The ground for disagreement is about the limit which brings a rise in the rate of investment to a halt. Why does not a small initial impulse produce an indefinite upswing in investment?

(a) The Financial Limit.

Can a limit be found in the supply of finance? A rise in national income causes an increased demand for money, and so drives up the rate of interest, and an over-rapid drain on the pool of finance exhausts it, so that, after a certain time, there are insufficient funds available to be borrowed, and new schemes of investment cease to be made. An explanation on these lines is plausible enough when we are discussing a boom in one part of an inter-national trading system. A relative boom causes diffi-culties in the balance of payments of the booming country,

[1] Kalecki [16], "A Theory of the Business Cycle", and "The 'Pure' Business Cycle " [17]. Mr. Kaldor's " Model of the Trade Cycle " [14], *Economic Journal*, March 1940, belongs to the same family. That of Mr. Hicks [9] has some resemblance to it, but is excessively vague about the main point—the relation of capacity to the demand for output. R. M. Goodwin (Econometrics in Business-Cycle Analysis [6a], a chapter in Alvin Hansen, *Business Cycles and National Income*) reworks Kalecki's theory with capacity instead of finance as the short-period bottleneck. His point of view is therefore pretty well identical with mine. This light is hidden under a bushel, and I did not see it until the present work was completed.

which have to be corrected by credit restriction, as under traditional bank-rate policy.

But when the boom is spread evenly over the world, so that we can treat the world as a single economy, it is hard to see why finance should check the upswing, for the financial bottle has an elastic neck. There is no reason why the banking system, in a closed economy, should not "meet the needs of trade" and allow the supply of money to expand as required, and even if the rate of interest does rise as a boom develops, the cost of borrowing to entrepreneurs is likely to fall, as their own confidence in future profits communicates itself to the other side of the market for loans.[1]

Moreover, a boom is a time of high profits, and an abnormal proportion of saving is being made directly by entrepreneurs (all the more so if money-wage rates, and with them prices, are rising, robbing the rentiers to the benefit of net profit). Thus the pool of potential finance is more likely to be filling up than draining away.[2]

Financial stringency, indeed, may set in with great violence when profit expectations fail, but that means that finance kicks the boom when it is down, not that it knocks it over.

(b) Expectations.

Another kind of explanation is looked for in the reaction of expectations about the future to current experience. When profits are running round about their average of the past few years, this theory suggests, entrepreneurs have confidence in them, and then investment plans respond to each rise in the rate of profit. But when profits have grown far above the average, they feel it is too good to last. Thus, above a certain level, each increment

[1] Cf. below, p. 157. [2] Cf. above, p. 19 note.

in the rate of profit brings a smaller increment of investment plans, until the rate of investment ceases to increase, and the boom collapses.[1]

This theory seems plausible. And yet it is not very satisfactory, for if entrepreneurs held these views just a little more strongly, there would be no boom at all. The amplification of the original upswing in investment was due to the fact that entrepreneurs expected the new level of demand to hold for long enough to make it worth their while to enlarge their productive capacity. If each one said to himself: "Don't be had for a mug; this is only a boom", he would enjoy the raised demand while it lasted, but would not lay down new plant. The original rise in investment would not amplify itself, and the boom would be reduced to a ripple. Thus this theory seems to require that entrepreneurs' expectations of the future should react just enough and not too much to improved profits in the present. (It also suggests that the more books they read about the trade cycle, the weaker booms will become.)

(c) *Full Employment.*

According to another line of argument, the boom ceases to grow (and therefore falls off) when it runs up against full employment. Since full employment is the ultimate bottleneck, and expansion can go no further once it has been reached (or rather cannot then exceed the pace at which output per man increases) it is obvious that something or other is bound to stop expansion if it gets there. But it is by no means obvious through what mechanism full employment can bring a boom to an end, and we must examine the matter more closely.

Let us suppose that fixed equipment is unimportant, and

[1] Kalecki [16], p. 135.

finance no object. Labour is the inner bottleneck. A boom has reached full employment while its impetus is still strong—that is to say the total increment to the stock of capital that entrepreneurs have it in mind to make is large relatively to a year's national income.

Now if labour is highly mobile between industries, there is no limit to the pace at which investment plans can be carried out (except the mere technical impossibility of doing everything at once).

At first money-wage rates remain unchanged. Prices have risen compared to what they were before full employment was reached, the real purchasing power, and consequently the rate of consumption, of workers and rentiers has been reduced, and the labour so released from consumption-good industries has been absorbed into investment; the shift to profit due to the rise in prices relatively to money wages ensures a rate of saving equivalent to the outlay on investment. (This is the phenomenon sometimes described as "forced saving".) So long as money wages are held constant there is no limit to this process. But the further it goes (the more rapid the pace at which investment plans are carried out) the lower are real wages, and at some point a rise in money-wage rates will have to be granted. When it is, either prices immediately rise further, so that a new rise in wages has to be granted, or, if wages are allowed to catch up for a moment, consumption recovers; the entrepreneurs in consumption-good industries are then anxious to get their workers back, and begin to bid for them. In either case the vicious spiral sets in, leading to hyper-inflation (unless we call in the financial limit to bring the story to an end). Thus over-all full employment is not so much a bottleneck as a powder barrel.[1]

[1] Cf. [35], p. 17.

But this is the image of war, famine or rearmament. Ordinary booms rarely seem to run into hyper-inflation. The reason is, no doubt, that normally there is enough labour awaiting employment to give a boom all the scope that it can use. Unless industry has been expanding relatively to population for some time past, arrears have silted up and there is a pool of disguised unemployment to draw upon. And while a boom is going on the population is increasing, and labour-saving innovations are reducing the demand for labour relatively to output. Thus a boom would have first to devour the reserve and then to catch up with the growth in supply of labour, before it had absorbed all the unemployment and come to the point where labour in general sets a limit to expansion.

True, where there are certain key men of special skill required for the investment industries, investment reaches its physical maximum when they are all employed. But it could be only by a lucky accident of history that at the level of investment so determined there was general full employment. From an analytical, though not from a human, point of view, the supply of skill is analogous to the supply of fixed equipment, and the limit which it sets to investment works in the same way.[1]

(d) Full Capacity.

How does capacity set a limit to the rate of investment? A scheme of investment has three dimensions (this is a point which is not always made clear in trade-cycle theory). A given piece of construction requires a certain rate of investment per week to be carried out, for a certain number of weeks. Once an entrepreneur has decided, say, to lay down a new plant, he would no doubt like the investment to be carried out as fast as possible. The actual

[1] See above, p. 23.

rate at which it will be carried out depends partly on technical considerations and partly upon the state of the order books of the contractors who undertake it. When an entrepreneur in a construction trade is offered orders that more than fill his capacity, he does not choke back the excess demand by raising prices, for if he kills off a lump of demand he has lost it for good. He may raise his prices somewhat, but his chief method of rationing out his limited capacity is to slow down deliveries.

We can see how this affects the rate of investment by means of a stylised example. We call successive periods by the names of the months (giving each four weeks only) though the time periods involved in an actual case may be supposed much longer than literal months. The rate of investment apart from that shown in the example is assumed constant throughout the story.

Value of scheme		Investment per week	Period of gestation		
A	240	10	24 weeks,		Jan.–June
B	256	8	32	,,	Feb.–Sept.
C	160	5	32	,,	Mar.–Oct.
D	72	2	36	,,	Apr.–Dec.
E	60	Not begun	—		—

Some initial cause has led to the drawing of a blue-print for scheme A, an installation whose total cost is represented by 240 units. Work begins upon it in January, raising the total rate of investment in the economy by 10 per week above its December value. The consequent increase in effective demand calls into being scheme B, of 256 units. (The value of the schemes is deliberately made arbitrary, for once we have left our mythical steady economy there is no reason to expect any simple relationship between an increase in demand and the value of the capacity designed to meet it.)

This situation is highly "explosive", for the first scheme of investment has induced a further demand for new equipment greater than itself. But the construction trades were already booming, and they cannot work on scheme B at a greater rate than 8 per week. A rise of 8 in investment, begun in February, calls out a further increase of 5 in March, which leads to 2 more in April. Now, at 25 per week, the construction industries cannot begin on any fresh orders, and scheme E is kept waiting. From the beginning of April till the end of June construction is running at its peak, and general prosperity rules. But at the end of June scheme A is completed. Even if it were feasible to switch all the capacity thereby released immediately to speeding up the completion of the other schemes (or taking E out of the queue) investment would continue at its peak only a few months longer. (Say, B is completed in August.) No rise in income occurs after April, and no new plans are laid. And meanwhile, from July onwards, A is in operation and is competing for demand wherever its market may be, and lowering the average of profits there. The "explosive" upswing has "damped" itself to a standstill.

We have tacitly assumed that although the capital-good entrepreneurs are enjoying a seller's market, there are not enough orders in sight to justify them in enlarging their own capacity. If they were doing so, the boom might take on a second lease of life. Suppose that scheme A is providing capacity to meet the needs of E, now waiting in the queue (say, E is a fleet of ships and A a shipyard). Then in July, when A is ready to begin work, investment in E (combined, perhaps with a speeding up of B, C and

D) raises the rate of investment by more than the amount lost through the completion of A. (The economy has now broken through to a higher level of constructional activity than any known, at least in the recent past, for the capacity of the capital-good industries registers the rate of investment that they have formerly catered for.) The increase in income from June to July calls still more schemes into being. But (except in a freakishly "explosive" case) the new schemes are not sufficient both to keep the now enlarged investment capacity running, and to re-place E in the queue. It follows that if the same process were gone through again, and investment capacity increased a second or a third time, there would not be enough uncompleted schemes to make use of it, and no further rise in the rate of investment would occur. Thus, if not sooner then later, a moment comes when the completion of a batch of schemes reduces the current rate of investment by more than the commencement of work on new schemes makes good.

When the rate of investment falls, the rate of profit falls, and expectations suffer a shock. Outstanding orders may then be cancelled, so that the rate of investment drops abruptly, or they may be worked off so that the rate of investment moves down step by step as it rose. Abruptly or gradually, income falls with investment, leaving surplus capacity high and dry as it ebbs.

The causation of fluctuations is infinitely complex, and no doubt there is room in attempting to explain it for elements of all the theories mentioned above (and more as well) but I want to suggest that the explanation of the upper turning point of a boom which is both the simplest and the most in accord with experience is to be found in the limited capacity (at any given moment of time) of the capital-goods industries, and that its simple essence is shown in the above example, however intricate its detailed manifestations may be.

II. A SCARCITY OF LABOUR

We have argued that full employment is likely to be an uncommon state of affairs, but clearly it is not impossible in principle. Let us examine a situation where population is constant and where there is no reserve army in disguised unemployment and no surplus agricultural labour awaiting a chance to get into industry; it so happens (as a result of past development) that the number of workers and the capacity of capital just about coincide. Now a boom occurs; output rises from somewhere below capacity to just above it. This is made possible by over-time working and by scraping the barrel for "unemploy-ables" to take into service. After a short time, capacity is increased (as completed investment schemes come off the stocks) but we will suppose that the queue of un-completed constructional projects is still large, so that the boom is continuing. Now in this situation entrepreneurs find themselves in a seller's market, and they have capacity to produce, but they cannot find hands. There is not the perfect mobility of labour and indefinite investment demand that was described above where labour was the only bottleneck, and it is not inevitable that a vicious spiral should set in. Wages may be raised, but let us suppose there are sufficient frictions and stickiness in the system to save it from plunging into hyper-inflation. Yet there is excess demand for labour. The entrepreneurs cannot get all the output for which they see demand clamouring around them. It would be very unnatural to suppose that they just lie down and leave these excellent profit opportunities to run to waste. Rather they take great pains to increase output per man. New labour-saving devices are sought for, devices already known are introduced into formerly "backward" plants, and the slack which exists in even the best ones in normal times is pulled in. This experience may give a permanent twist to technical progress, and set competition between firms going on a permanently higher level, so that even when the boom is over technical progress continues at a faster pace than formerly.

It will be recalled that we examined an economy where growth of population had recently come to an end, and found it to fall into a slump. The reason was that its former rate of rise in output per head was not sufficient to maintain its former rate of accumulation, so that it needed ever more consumers to keep its growing stock of capital profitably employed. When population growth ceased a slump set in, there was unemployment and no special reason to save labour.

It now seems that if the economy had ridden into this situation on the back of a strong boom (that is, with effective demand straining the limits of capacity) instead of reaching it when only a mild "normal" impulse to accumulate (with output at best keeping up with capacity) had been ruling over the past few years, the whole situation would be completely different. The prospective fall in demand, due to the cessation of population growth, has no effect, for it is swamped by the existing boom conditions, but the scarcity of hands makes itself felt immediately, and sets productivity rising at a faster pace than formerly prevailed. Thus it depends upon an historical accident whether the cessation of population growth is a misfortune or a blessing to a private enterprise economy.

"This was sometime a paradox, but now the time gives it proof."

III. BOOM AND TREND

When, owing to general uncertainty, present experience is heavily weighted in the formation of expectations about the future, any of the vicissitudes which we found to accelerate accumulation in a developing economy gives rise to a boom. The boom may be of any magnitude, and prolonged to any length of time, according to the strength of the initial impulse and the extent of its repercussions in inducing further accumulation to be planned.

One of the great boosts which we referred to above (such as occurs when railway building opens up a new territory) may give rise to a linked series of booms. Accumulation, rushing at the investment opportunities offered, over-shoots the expansion of demand and the first boom is checked; but the existence of the capacity created in the first boom opens up fresh investment opportunities (say, farmers have settled in the hinterland on each side of the trunk line and it soon seems profitable to build branch lines out of them). After a pause for digestion the boom starts up again.[1]

However a boom may develop, it can never find a steady path to follow, for it is based upon self-contradictory assumptions. The essence of a boom is that output is high relatively to capacity, and investment schemes are being planned in the hope of enjoying the high profits of a seller's market which they are themselves bound to destroy.

While a boom goes on, the long-period forces are at work, increasing productivity. Provided that long-period thriftiness is not increasing, total consumption is creeping up as output per man-hour and the real purchasing power of an hour's labour are rising. Thus a permanent increase

[1] Cf. Keirstead [18], p. 143.

in the rate of consumption is going on, in the sense that the rate of consumption corresponding to a given rate of investment is greater at a later date than at an earlier one. This provides a permanent use for a part of the capacity created during the boom. Thus, the boom is partly justified by the trend. Or rather the boom is part of the trend. A lump of accumulation, which, if it had been made at a steady pace, would have taken longer, but could have been continued, is crammed into a short space of time and then interrupted.

In the "under-consumptionist" case, when long-run thriftiness is rising as time goes by (owing, say, to a falling share of labour in product) so that the passage of time reduces consumption corresponding to a given rate of investment, or when there has been a cessation of population growth, or a slowing down in the rate of technical progress, the breakdown of a boom leaves capacity which cannot ever find a profitable market for its product. Thus a downturn in the trend shows itself in a deepening and prolongation of the first slump that happens after it has occurred.

Our argument is conducted in terms of output as a whole, without regard to the effects of different rates of development in different lines of production. In reality each industry is subject to its own vicissitudes, and each boom is coloured by the character of the particular industries whose development dominates it.[1] This is of great importance and cannot be neglected in historical analysis. But our argument is designed to show that the basic mechanism of economic fluctuations does not depend upon disproportionalities in the development of different industries, and would be at work even in an economy

---

[1] Cf. Rostow, " Some Notes on Mr. Hicks and History " [37], *American Economic Review*, June 1951.

where all lines of production were affected in the same proportion.

IV. THE END OF A SLUMP

A slump is a situation in which output has fallen sharply below capacity. Depression then lasts until the surplus capacity disappears and investment can revive. The General Theory was developed in terms of this situation, and there is no need to dwell upon its characteristics here, but we must link it to our long-term analysis by inquiring how it comes to an end.

We will not consider a slump which is a mere hiccup between linked booms, nor one which marks the onset of secular stagnation, but consider a depression of an intermediate type, which consists in a fall in the rate of accumulation below the average experienced for some time past, with a constant long-run average propensity to consume. How does such a slump come to an end?

It would be begging the question to say that the trend lifts the economy out of depression a certain time after a slump has occurred, for the trend is accumulation, and the question is how accumulation starts going again.

Growing population is one source of expanding demand, for we found that, to a small extent at least, unemployed workers do eat themselves into jobs. And we found that a growth in demand from agriculture (whether it is part of the capitalist system or the output of pioneers from the reserve army opening up new territory for themselves) keeps industry expanding. Changes in relative demands (particularly a change in favour of housing) gives rise to investment opportunities even when total consumption is constant.

When none of these forces is at work, where can we look for hope of a revival? The mere fact that the run down in output must stop somewhere causes a bounce back from the bottom of a downswing, for when output ceases to fall, secondary disinvestment in work-in-progress comes to an end. Where the stock of capital is mainly working capital (plant is unimportant) this might be sufficient by itself to start a revival. But where long-lived equipment is a great proportion of capital and construction the main ingredient in investment, this is not enough, for the kick-back still leaves idle industrial capacity, which undermines the inducement to invest in more.

Where the slump so much discourages entrepreneurs that they fail to make good wear and tear, the stock of capital gradually shrinks. Here we find another of the paradoxes of expectations, for if the entrepreneurs believe that the depression is going to be long, they cut renewals further, or cease them altogether, and so shorten the slump by making it deeper for a time, while if they believe it will be short, they prolong it. A slump which everyone kept on expecting to end next year, might go on for ever.

Given that renewals fall off, the time which it takes for the stock of capital to shrink partly depends upon its age composition. If it happened that a large proportion of plant was reaching the end of its usable life when the slump set in, there would be a drastic fall in capacity, and therefore a rise in prospective profits, at an early stage in the depression. This is the way in which a former boom echoes itself in a revival of gross investment.[1] In the contrary case, where the bulk of plant was created in the recent past, the depression must continue for a long time before shrinkage begins to be appreciable.

Where the age distribution of plant is uniform, so that when capital is being worked to capacity a regular proportion is renewed every year, the proportion of

[1] See above, p. 58.

renewals is a function of the length of life of plant. Thus if the length of life is ten years, ten per cent. is replaced every year. It does not follow, however, that in such a case capacity would shrink by ten per cent. per annum when renewals ceased, for the shrinkage of capacity is slowed down by slump conditions (unless monopolistic machine-smashing is organised). Plant is worked less intensively so that wear and tear is reduced; in general the older plant will be put into store and the newest kept running; and there is a tendency when the future is doubtful to "make do" with old plant, which in prosperous conditions would have been scrapped and superseded. Thus, even if renewals cease altogether, the rate at which the stock of capital shrinks is likely to be very slow.

Meanwhile demand, at a given level of income, may be rising. There is ground for dispute whether the genial atmosphere of a boom or the desperate competition of a slump is the more conducive to innovations (though there can be little doubt that a slump combined with agreements to restrict competition is unconducive to progress). However that may be, some technical progress goes on during the depression. Let us suppose that money-wage rates are constant throughout the story. Prices fell when the slump set in, raising real-wage rates (this was one of the factors which brought the downswing to a halt). From now on, prices fall further as technical progress goes on (unless this tendency is fully offset by growing monopoly). The consequent rise in the real wage per man-hour, from the point of view of the workers, is partly or wholly offset by technological unemployment, so that real earnings do not rise correspondingly. But the real purchasing power of rentier incomes is increased by it (provided that their money incomes have not been too much cut by bankruptcies and "axing" of salaries) and so the level of consumption corresponding to a given level of investment is gradually raised.

Thus consumption creeps in this petty pace to meet a slowly shrinking capacity. Somewhere the two movements cross, surplus capacity disappears, the rate of profit returns to its normal level, and the stage is set for a revival of investment.

But after this bad experience, the mechanism by which a revival of investment induces further schemes of investment must be supposed to be enfeebled. Certainly it will be a long time before the investment industries want to enlarge their capacity. If the system has nothing but its own inherent buoyancy to rely upon, it seems as though the revival, when at last it comes, will be much weaker than the boom which preceded it.

In those theories which purport to find a cyclical mechanism in a private enterprise economy, I have the impression that the weakest chapter is always the one which treats of revival from a depression. And it seems to me that this is no accident. I take leave to doubt (though with all due hesitation and reserve) whether there ever has been a trade *cycle*—that is, a self-perpetuating cyclical movement, as opposed to a series of fluctuations due to the propensity of a private enterprise economy to exaggerate its response, either way, to the chances and changes of history as it meets them.

It seems to me that the most plausible theory of the revival is Mr. Micawber's: given time, something will turn up. That is to say that a depression will not last for ever because some fresh opportunity for investment is bound to present itself sooner or later.

Or if it does not, policy takes a hand. But then the General Theory becomes a part of the subject matter that it has to investigate, and the argument moves on to a different plane.

NOTES ON THE ECONOMICS OF TECHNICAL PROGRESS

NOTES ON THE ECONOMICS OF
TECHNICAL PROGRESS

TECHNICAL progress is a large subject, involving the whole history of the human race. We are here concerned only with changes of methods of production in a developed capitalist system, and our argument will apply to piecemeal innovations, not to great technical revolutions which transform a whole society and make comparisons between its present and its former state more or less meaningless.

I. INTRODUCTION

In the conventional marginal-productivity system of analysis it is taken for granted that, "in a given state of knowledge", there is a continuous series of combinations of factors of production which can be used to produce a given output. Then production is carried on with the combination which minimises costs, given the prices of the factors. A change in relative factor prices alters the combination chosen. An invention increases knowledge, on this view, and in the new state of knowledge there is again the possibility of continuous variation in the proportions of factors employed. The distinction between inventions which increase knowledge and adaptations to changes in factor prices, however, is by no means easy to draw, either in principle or in practice.[1] Here we make no use of it, but speak instead (using Schumpeter's term) of *innovations*, which are changes in methods of production, whether due to new inventions or to any other change in

[1] See below, p. 99.

79

circumstances. With each method of production there is one combination of factors required for a given output, and an innovation involves stepping from one combination to another. It is obvious that innovations may be made in response to changes in the price or availability of factors—as now in England productivity per man hour is being raised in response to scarcity of labour—but we shall treat them in just the same way as those which result from technical discoveries and the by-products of scientific development. The relation of this point of view to the traditional analysis is discussed below.[1]

2. The Impact of an Innovation

An entrepreneur may introduce a new method of production in order to enter a market debarred to him with existing techniques (for instance by patents) or to increase his hold upon a market by giving himself some monopolistic advantage, or to exploit a monopsonistic position by cheapening the factors he employs. In such cases the new method of production is not necessarily an improvement on the old from any point of view except his own. We shall confine our discussion to innovations which are introduced in the first place in order to save cost per unit of proceeds. We reckon costs at the factor prices ruling at the moment when the innovation is introduced.

An entrepreneur, let us suppose, introduces a new method of production which he expects to lower his manufacturing costs; or which, by making the product more marketable, lowers his selling costs; or which enables him to convince his customers that the product of the new method is an improvement on existing commodities and so to charge a higher price for it. The price

[1] See below, p. 100.

of the product is fixed in relation to the prices of its closest substitutes (a little less to gain a competitive advantage, a little more to exploit demand for a new quality). Even if the product is quite different from any known before (not a mere substitute, like rayon or nylon) it still must belong to some wide category of commodities meeting human wants, say, for food, transport, amusement or snobbery, and its price can be set in the light of the prices of competitive commodities, though the relation may not be very close to any one of them.

The innovation being successful, the entrepreneur now enjoys net receipts from a given outlay higher than those of similar producers using old techniques.

If the innovator has some advantage which other entrepreneurs do not enjoy (apart from being the first to use the new method) his profits are likely to continue greater than theirs. But if the new method is open to all, then rivals of the innovator, pressed by his competition or attracted by the spectacle of his profits, imitate his method, perhaps after a period of losses or low profits while they continue to use the now obsolete technique. Sooner or later, price is reduced towards the new level of costs.[1] If the industry is competitive, in the broad sense, excess profits are eliminated, and the innovator (unless he has meanwhile gone on to something fresh) after a time is back where he was.

It might appear that he could have saved himself a great deal of trouble by never making the innovation. But he has enjoyed abnormal profits for a certain time. Moreover, he may have believed that if he did not

[1] Exponents of the "full-cost" theory of pricing might argue that price is fixed at this level in the first place; but, if so, the innovator would be under-selling all his competitors, and, unless productive capacity at his disposal was immediately raised sufficiently to meet the whole demand for his product, he would have to ration his customers.

make the innovation, someone else would, so that in the end he would have been compelled to introduce it all the same, without the advantage of having been the leader.[1] (Since the fear of loss is more powerful than the hope of gain, it seems likely that cost-saving innovations are more rapidly made in competitive industries than by monopolists—other things equal.)

3. DEFINITIONS

Technical progress is difficult to discuss in precise language. We have no definite unit on which to reckon the quantities concerned. Commodities alter their character, capital equipment its form, labour its productivity and money its purchasing power. Yet the problem is not metaphysical. Actual business men make actual innovations to save actual costs, and actual effects follow therefrom. A craven scruple of thinking too precisely on the definitions must not prevent us from trying to analyse them. It seems better to hack a way through the problem by making drastic simplifications, and then to adapt the argument to complicated cases as best we may.

1. We will confine the discussion to innovations in the production of a definite homogeneous commodity, which is not altered in any way by changes in the technique of producing it. This assumption is retained throughout the argument. It is necessary in order to give a criterion for a change in costs, for if commodities change their nature (as indeed they often do) with their methods of production, it is hard

[1] This view of the process of innovation is derived from Marx *via* Schumpeter. It seems to correspond to experience better than any other.

to say whether they have become cheaper or merely nastier as a result. It follows that all applications of the analysis to actual cases must necessarily be somewhat vague. This is the vagueness which always clouds the conception of real income or real productivity.

2. There is no monopsony in the market for factors of production.

3. There are no economies of large-scale industry.

4. There are no scarce factors of production.

5. The costs of production of the commodity are calculated for the rate of output at which plant is working normally—not at the absolute physical limit of capacity, with no reserve, but at the rate of working for which it was designed. This is described as capacity output. Similarly the cost of equipment is reckoned at the capacity output of plants producing it. We are concerned, that is to say, with long-period normal costs.[1] (In reality innovations follow on each other's heels faster than adjustment is reached to any one, and a great number of techniques are being used, with varying rates of profits, at any moment, in any one industry, so that the actual average rate of profit realised partly depends upon the rate at which innovations are made relatively to the time taken to digest them.)

These assumptions entail that demand has no influence upon normal price, except in so far as it acts through changes in the degree of competition in the market for the commodity.

[1] Where there are technical economies of scale—the cost of plant per unit of output varies with capacity output—an innovation which reduces cost per unit of output when output is large might raise it if output were

Before we can go any further there is an awkward complication to be dealt with. Cost from the point of view of any one firm partly depends upon the prices at which raw material, power and equipment can be bought from other firms, and these prices depend not only on their costs of production but also on the rate of net profit in the firms which sell them. We will put this point on one side for the moment by postulating completely integrated firms carrying out the whole process of production of a particular commodity, each having a department producing the equipment that it requires. (This would rarely be found in reality—it is merely an expository device.)

Since capital goods are produced by labour with the aid of capital goods in an endless circle (we are abstracting from scarce factors of production), all costs can be reduced to current labour, labour expended on the initial cost of capital goods, and interest on the value locked up in capital goods.

All costs can be reckoned in terms of wage units. (This involves an index-number problem. Differences in wages rates for different types of labour can be dealt with simply by averaging, but when wage rates vary relatively to each other as technical change goes on our unit of measurement becomes unreliable.) The labour cost of a given rate of output then reduces to the man-hours worked in producing it, weighting hours by the wage rate commanded by the type of labour concerned. The capital cost consists of interest at the current rate on the quantity of capital required, with the technique in use, to produce that rate

---

smaller. We calculate average cost when the rate of output is sufficient to keep plant running at capacity with either technique. (Whether the old or the new technique involves the larger capacity output for a plant may have an important influence on the degree of competition; see below, p. 92.)

of output. The quantity of capital is a physical entity—the actual equipment and work-in-progress required for the given rate of output. To reduce it to terms comparable with the quantity of labour it must be measured by the number of wage units which represent its normal cost of production. (This is not the same thing as the labour cost of the capital goods concerned, for it includes also interest on the capital goods required to produce them.)

There is another element in cost which raises further complications. Commodities are, so to speak, charged with reproducing their own capital and, both in business practice and in social accounting, replacement of capital is properly regarded as entering into the cost of production of commodities.

The replacement cost of capital goods used up in the process of production can be eliminated, so far as working capital is concerned, by reckoning a year's output after replacing work-in-progress at the beginning of the year.

Long-lived plant cannot be dealt with so easily. The capacity output of given plant is two-dimensional. It consists of a certain rate of output per year, for a certain number of years. Thus we must include in the cost of a year's output an amortisation charge calculated to return the cost of plant over its working life. In a changing world, this necessarily contains an element of estimation or convention, for it depends upon the length of future useful life expected for the plant. This makes the calculation of net output vague and ambiguous. The best that we can do is to say that net proceeds are the year's receipts *minus* estimated amortisation costs, and net physical output is the year's output reduced in the ratio of net to gross proceeds. A reduction in amortisation charges then reduces the cost of the commodity by raising the ratio of net to gross output for a given outlay. This is a somewhat awkward device, but it causes trouble only when the expected length of life of plant is changing.

On this basis, the cost of a given rate of net output consists only of labour cost and capital cost. The excess of proceeds over costs is net profit. Profit, *simpliciter*, is the total return on capital, that is, interest *plus* net profit.

4. CATEGORIES OF INNOVATIONS

We may now proceed to discuss the way in which these elements in cost may be affected by innovations.

The simplest approach to this problem is to begin by examining the proposition that an equal proportional increase in output per man-hour in all departments saves capital cost and labour cost in equal proportions.[1] Clearly, this holds good so long as the type of labour employed and the physical nature of the capital goods required for a given rate of output remain unchanged, and the length of life of plant and the rate of turnover of working capital are constant. In these conditions, an increase, in a given proportion, in output per man-hour at all stages of production reduces the cost of working capital and of plant, for a given rate of output, in the same proportion as it reduces labour cost.

Where production passes through a number of stages the cost incurred at the earlier stage is carried for a longer time than at the finishing stages, so that an increase in output per man-hour at an early stage of production reduces the cost of the capital represented by work-in-progress by more than a proportionate increase at a later stage.

When output per machine is given, an innovation

[1] See "The Classification of Inventions" [34], *Review of Economic Studies*, February 1938, and Harrod, *Towards a Dynamic Economics* [8], p. 23.

which increases output per man-hour equally in minding machines and in making machines reduces capital cost in the same proportion as labour cost. An improvement in machine making only, saves capital more than labour, and in machine minding only, saves labour more than capital.

Thus, so long as the physical quantity and the physical nature of the capital goods required to produce a given rate of output are unchanged, it is a simple matter to say how an innovation affects the elements in cost.

But obviously most innovations cannot be fitted into this formula, for usually the physical capital required for a given rate of output is changed as technique alters.

Even apart from changes in the design of plant there are many ways in which physical capital per unit of output may alter. A speeding up of the processes of production reduces the physical amount of goods in the pipeline for a given annual output, and reduces capital cost without directly affecting labour cost. Where the ratio of men to machines is fixed an improvement in their performance reduces the number of machines required for a given output in the same proportion as it reduces man-hours of labour. The introduction of a multiple-shift system with plant and technique otherwise unchanged reduces the plant required for a given output and so saves capital cost while leaving labour cost unchanged.

Moreover, innovations are often worth making even if they raise one element in cost, provided that they reduce other elements by more. Innovations which increase labour cost may be made when capital has become scarce relatively to what it was in the recent past (it was suggested that men with bicycles should replace coal and locomotives in the Rhineland railways in 1945) or when an increase in riskiness or a rise in the rate of interest has discouraged the use of capital. More often it pays to increase capital cost in order to save labour cost, as when unskilled machine-minders take the place of craftsmen.

Innovations may save amortisation charges, or may raise them as a result of saving other elements in cost. It may be worth while to make a change which lengthens the physical life of plant, or which reduces the risk of obsolescence by taking a long jump forward in technique, even if it requires an increase in initial cost of plant, and therefore heavier interest charges. Or it may be worth while to save initial cost, even at the expense of making plant less durable. Such changes are likely to affect labour costs also, for instance by causing less or more time to be lost on account of mechanical breakdowns, since plant which is longer lived may be less fragile.

Thus the influence of innovations on costs is too various to be fitted into a simple formula in terms of stages of production.

Capital, however (with the reservations noted above), can be measured in terms of the cost in wage units of the outfit of capital goods required to produce a given rate of output, and a reduction in capital per unit of output can be treated in the same way, whether it is due to a physical change in the capital goods required or to a fall in the cost of physically unchanged capital goods, or to any mixture of the two.

On this basis, all types of innovations can be described in terms of the changes in the quantities of labour and capital required to produce a given rate of output, and it is on this basis that our argument will be conducted.

It is often supposed that the nature of technical development is generally such as to increase the use of capital. But there is little ground for this opinion. The commonest kind of innovation, the mechanisation of production, usually increases capital cost in respect of plant. But at the same time it speeds up production and reduces capital cost in respect to work-in-progress. It may be doubted whether even the introduction of the railways, which seem at a casual glance to have made a spectacular increase in the use of capital, really did so very much. A railway with its rolling stock obviously contains more capital than a train of pack mules, but it may have reduced the amount of goods in the pipeline necessary to supply a given market from the equivalent of the consumption of several months to the consumption of a few days. In general, there does not seem to be any particular presumption that innovations save capital any less than they save labour.

5. REAL WAGES

The next question to be discussed is the effect of technical progress upon wage rates. A saving in labour cost due to an increase in output per man-hour by a given type of labour is totally different in its effects from a saving due to using a cheaper type of labour. We will at first assume that all labour is alike. Labour employed is then measured simply in uniform man-hours of work. We will assume that the rate of interest remains constant throughout the story.

Let us first consider a case where the money-wage rate per man-hour does not alter. Then the effect of innovations on the wage in terms of product depends entirely on what happens to the price of the commodity. If the price of the commodity remains where it was, the wage per man-hour in terms of product remains unchanged, however much productivity has increased. Innovations, whatever form they take, then raise net profit per unit of output, and they raise the rate of profit per unit of capital unless the innovation has required an increase in capital per unit of output proportionate to the rise in profit per unit of output.

But to maintain the price of the commodity constant when money costs have fallen implies a complete absence of competition. Let us consider a case where the force of competition is sufficient to reduce net profit per unit of capital to its former level after the innovation has taken place (this requires that there are a number of potential competitors who command sufficient finance to make investment in capacity of the most efficient size), and let us look at the position when the innovation has been diffused throughout the industry producing the commodity concerned, and any necessary investment has been completed. Then competition has reduced the price of the commodity to equality with the new level of costs *plus* net profit per unit of capital at the former rate. The same result is reached when price is constant and excess profits are eliminated by a rise in money wages, or in any intermediate case.

Now, an innovation which reduces capital cost and labour cost in the same proportion, with a constant rate of profit on capital, reduces price in terms of wage units in the same proportion in which output per man-hour has risen.

When labour per unit of output is reduced more than capital (*a fortiori* when capital per unit of output is increased) total cost is reduced in a smaller proportion than labour cost; the wage in terms of product then rises less than in proportion to net output per man-hour. Conversely, an innovation which saves capital more than labour reduces price and raises the wage in terms of product more than in proportion to the rise in net output per man-hour. (Even if the innovation saved capital cost at the expense of raising labour cost, so that output per man-hour fell, it would still raise the wage in terms of product, for it would reduce total cost, and therefore price.)

This system of ideas can be applied to a single commodity in isolation. It can be applied to total output if we imagine a "one-commodity world" in which all products are alike in respect to their conditions of production (no need to strain imagination by supposing that there is only one commodity from the point of view of consumers). In a one-commodity world a rise in wages in terms of product is a rise in real wages in the ordinary sense. When an innovation affects one industry in isolation, a rise in wages in terms of its product is a rise in real wages only in so far as the product enters into the consumption of the workers.

If we imagine all industries except one to be enjoying innovations, then real wages in that industry must be supposed to rise, no less than in the rest. With all money wage rates constant, all prices except that of the industry where technique is stationary fall; or if prices remain constant, the stationary industry must raise its money-wage rates moie or less in step with the others, in order to retain its labour force. In either case (or in any intermediate case) the price of the commodity in terms of other commodities is rising as time goes by, and where the commodity is an important one (say, housing) it retards the rise in real wage rates due to the general progress of technique. If it is not indispensable, it sinks into the position of a luxury trade or disappears from use altogether.

As soon as we step outside the shelter of our assumptions and conceive of an economy in which different types of innovations affect different products, it is necessary to evaluate the relative importance, in some sense, of innovations in different industries, and the index-number problem clouds all calculations. But it seems safe enough to say that technical progress cannot fail to raise the real wage per man-hour provided that the rate of interest and the rate of net profit do not rise.

We must now remove the assumption that competition everywhere keeps the rate of net profit constant. An increase in the rate of profit per unit of capital in wage-good industries checks (and might even reverse) the rise in real wages due to technical progress. (A rise in profits in pure luxury trades merely makes capitalists pay each other's profits.)

Since in reality firms are not fully integrated, we must take account of purchases of equipment and materials by one firm from another. A rise in profits in the firms selling them counts twice over, for the element of net profit in the price of these goods reappears in cost of capital in the industries using them and receives interest and net profit over again.[1]

It often happens that innovations raise the minimum unit of investment required for production, and so tend to limit the possibility of entry into a trade. This automatically reduces the pressure of competition and may lead to a rise in the rate of net profit. The effect upon real wages then depends upon the significance of the commodities concerned in the consumption of the workers.

There is another aspect of the matter which is of great importance to the workers. Innovations, whether they save capital or not, normally save labour. That is to say, the number of man-hours of work required to produce a

[1] Mr. Kalecki's theory of the effect of monopoly on distribution thus gains force by being transferred into a long-period setting. "The Distribution of the National Income", *Essays in Economic Fluctuations* [16].

given output is continually falling as technical progress goes on. At the same time, provided that the rate of profit is not rising so much as to prevent the real wage rate from rising, the workers are in a position (if they are free to choose) to reduce the work which a man does without reducing his real income. This may be done partly by shortening the working week (with single-shift working, this raises capital cost, by reducing the capacity output of given plant, and so checks the rise in the wage per man-hour in terms of product) or by increasing holidays, so as to reduce man-hours of work per man-year; and partly by raising the school-leaving age, and lowering the age of retirement, so as to reduce man-hours of work per man-lifetime.

In so far as this fails to occur, technological unemployment will result from labour-saving innovations, unless effective demand for commodities and capital goods rises step by step with the rise in output per head.

We must now remove the assumption that there is only one type of labour. Provided that the real wage per hour is rising, that technological unemployment is avoided, and that new methods do not make conditions of work more unpleasant, innovations may be regarded as favourable to workers in general.[1] But they may be highly deleterious to particular groups of workers.

Consider the case where an innovation saves labour cost by using unskilled workers instead of craftsmen (it may increase capital cost, for machinery is substituted for skill, and this may outweigh any saving in working capital due to the speeding up of production). The craftsmen may be obliged to accept lower money wages when the demand for their services falls. If their wage falls relatively

---

[1] Abstracting from the effects of the process of transition from one technique to another.

to the price of the commodity (which itself tends to fall relatively to wages in general) the diffusion of the innovation may be checked, and the craftsmen may continue to work side by side with the new plants employing unskilled labour. But if the new cost is such that in order to maintain a footing the craftsmen would have to accept a wage per hour less than that being received by the unskilled workers who have supplanted them, it is unlikely that the supply of craftsmen will survive a generation. (Some may escape into the production of a luxury brand of the original commodity.)

6. RELATIVE SHARES

We may now turn to the famous question of *neutral* technical progress, which leaves the relative share of labour and capital in social income constant.[1]

The conception of the ratio of capital to labour involves, as we have seen, one index number problem when the relative wages of different types of workers vary, and another when the element of net profit entering into the price of capital goods sold by one entrepreneur to another changes with the technique of production, and it involves the perennial problem of the ratio of net to gross output. But let us suppose that the amount of labour and the cost in terms of wage units of the capital required for a given rate of output can be measured more or less satisfactorily. Then, provided that the rate of interest is unchanged and that the price of the product moves in such a way as to keep the rate of net profit constant (so that the rate of profit, in the sense in which we are using the phrase, is constant) it is obvious that an innovation which saves labour cost and capital cost in the same proportion leaves

[1] Cf. Harrod [8], p. 23.

the relative shares unchanged. Labour per unit of output, capital per unit of output in terms of wage units and the price of the commodity in terms of wage units all fall in the same proportion. Capital measured in terms of wage units then bears a constant ratio to labour employed.

Since the price of the commodity is such as to keep the rate of profit constant, the stock of capital measured in terms of product bears a constant ratio to output. The wage per man-hour, in terms of product, rises in proportion to the fall in man-hours per unit of output. Thus the relative shares do not alter.

An innovation which saves labour more than capital (say, an increase in output per man-hour in the finishing stages only[1]), increases capital per unit of output measured in terms of product, and increases the share of capital in net output. An innovation which saves capital more than labour (say, an innovation in the departments making equipment)[2] increases the share of labour.

An innovation which lengthens the expected life of plant, without altering its initial cost, does not affect the ratio of capital to output, but it raises the ratio of net income to total outlay, and, with a constant rate of profit, raises wages and profits equally in terms of product.

This is all very well so long as the rate of profit is constant. But when the rate of profit is changed in consequence of the change in methods of production, an innovation which keeps the shares constant is one which alters capital per unit of output, measured in terms of product, inversely to the rate of profit. For instance, if it so happens that the price of the commodity is held constant when costs fall, the wage in terms of product is constant and any innovation which reduces labour per unit of output increases the relative share of capital. The

[1] See above, p. 86.   [2] Ibid.

relative shares would then be constant only when the innovation was of the type which saves capital while leaving labour cost constant (the rate of profit per unit of capital then rises in the proportion in which capital per unit of output falls).

It seems best to call innovations *neutral* which reduce labour and capital (measured in wage units) per unit of output in the same proportion, whatever happens to the rate of profit. Then a neutral innovation is one which leaves the relative shares unchanged in the special case when the rate of profit is constant.[1]

It is tempting to call an innovation which reduces the share of capital at a constant rate of profit "capital saving" and one which increases it "capital using".[2] But then "labour saving" and "capital saving" would not be symmetrical terms, for it is natural to call an innovation labour saving when it increases output per man-hour, that is, when it saves labour absolutely, not relatively to capital. It is symmetrical therefore to call an innovation which reduces capital per unit of output measured in terms of wage units "capital saving" and one which increases it "capital using". We then need a fresh term for an innovation which saves capital, not only absolutely, but in a greater proportion than it saves labour.

We might call innovations which reduce capital per unit of labour "unfavourable to capital" and those which raise it "favourable to capital". But it is important to bear in mind that these terms apply to the effect of innovations on relative shares only when the rate of profit is constant.

In a one-product world, neutral technical progress with a constant rate of profit means that the value of the stock

---

[1] This is Mr. Harrod's point of view ([8], p. 26.)

[2] I have used these terms in this sense myself, e.g. [35], p. 96.

of capital in existence is always a constant number of years purchase of the stream of net output.[1] Then the shares of labour and capital in total real income are constant.

If once more we leave the shelter of our assumptions and consider a complex of innovations affecting different products differently, we can still say, in a rough way, that technical change is neutral if innovations favourable to capital in some industries are offset by sufficiently unfavourable innovations in others. Then, with a constant rate of profit, the shares of capital and labour in net social income are constant in terms of money, but changes in relative prices may alter them in terms of the commodities in which their recipients are interested.

7. THE INFLUENCE OF FACTOR PRICES

We must now try to take account of the influence of relative factor prices upon technique and to examine the relation between the foregoing argument and the conception of a production function.

In a given situation there may be a number of techniques known, requiring different combinations of labour and capital. Neglecting differences between entrepreneurs, in situation or in skill in management, and assuming that each commands finance sufficient for the investment required for a productive unit with any technique, entrepreneurs are assumed to choose from the known possibilities the technique which gives the lowest cost of production of a given commodity, at the ruling factor prices. (It is possible for several techniques, using different combinations of factors, to yield the same costs.)

How do differences in factor prices affect the technique

[1] Cf. Harrod [8], p. 27.

97

chosen? A lower level of money wage rates all round (the rate of interest being constant) reduces labour cost and capital cost[1] in the same proportion, and has no influence on the technique to be preferred.

A lower rate of interest (compared to a higher one, each having obtained long enough to be fully digested) reduces capital cost twice over, for it reduces the cost of equipment (by reducing the interest charge on capital-producing equipment) as well as reducing the charge on a given cost of equipment (but it may raise the amortisation charge on a given cost by reducing the earnings of amortisation reserves). With a lower rate of interest it may be advantageous to adopt techniques which use capital in order to save labour[2] (a technique, already known, which saved both would have been preferred at the higher rate of interest). The share of capital in net output is greater or less at the lower than at the higher rate of interest according as the increase in capital per unit of output is greater or less, proportionately, than the reduction in interest *plus* net profit per unit of capital. (A lower rate of interest alters the relative long-run normal prices of different commodities, having the greatest effect where capital per unit of output is greatest.)

A lower rate of net profit which entrepreneurs are willing to accept, such as might be found if competition were keener, does not directly affect the technique chosen to produce a given commodity in an integrated concern, for a change in price has no effect upon the relative costs of production with different techniques. But where entrepreneurs buy capital goods from each other, a fall in

[1] And the marginal cost of products requiring scarce factors.

[2] Where such a change in technique has been made we should say in our terminology that innovations have been made which have increased capital cost per unit of output, for we reckon costs, with the new and the old techniques, at the lower rate of interest.

the price of capital goods relatively to wage rates encourages the adoption of capital-using techniques. (A
change in the level of net profits causes differences in
relative prices of commodities similar to those due to a
difference in the rate of interest.)

Where there is a continuous series of already known
techniques it is possible to draw up something resembling
a conventional production function, showing the net outputs of a given amount of current labour with different
outfits of capital goods. This line of thought may be
useful for very broad comparisons between the productivity
of different economies at various levels of development,
but it could rarely be applied with exactitude, for there
are likely to be many gaps and twists in any series of
known techniques.

Moreover, the acquisition of technical knowledge is a
one-way process. A change in methods of production,
induced, say, by a fall in the rate of interest, may lead to
developments which make the new method economic even
when the rate of interest rises again. If the rate of interest
had never fallen, the new method might never have been
discovered, yet if it had been known all along, it would
have been profitable to use it before ever the rate of
interest fell.[1] Further, technical knowledge has meaning
only when it is actually applied, and application involves
learning the "know how" of using it. Even if an indus-
trialist is supplied with complete blue prints for a certain
method of production he, his managers, and his workers,
still have to learn the method and to adapt it to their
particular situation, and a change intended to take advantage of an alteration in relative factor prices may

[1] Cf. Hicks, *Theory of Wages* [11], p. 125. The distinction between inventions " induced " by a change in factor prices and an adaptation to a
change in " a given state of knowledge " is somewhat tenuous.

involve the re-design of plant and a period of "teething troubles" while a new method is learned, just as much as does a change intended to take advantage of a new discovery.[1]

A "change in methods of production in a given state of knowledge" is, strictly speaking, a contradiction in terms.

Where there are scarce factors of production a fresh layer of complication is introduced into the analysis. Their prices to the individual entrepreneur depend upon the total demand for them, and any change in the relative prices of commodities or in the distribution of income, due to an innovation, sets up repercussions, *via* changes in demand and changes in scarce factor prices, which require further changes in technique. In such cases, perhaps, the required readjustments can sometimes be made by continuous small steps. But if each technique requires the use of specialised plant which, once built, runs its life through at whatever profit it can earn, adjustment to a single change must be conceived to require a long (perhaps endless) process of trial and error, and the notion of a long-period normal price ceases to be of much use.

To translate between our classification of innovations and the conventional analysis is by no means an easy matter, for our system runs in terms of the cost of production with different techniques at a given rate of interest, whereas the conventional analysis runs in terms of the effect of an invention upon the marginal productivity of "a given amount of capital"[2] and no one ever makes it clear how capital is to be measured. (Our method of measuring capital in terms of the cost of the outfit of capital goods required by a given technique, of course,

[1] Cf. Keirstead, *The Theory of Economic Change* [18], p. 174 et seq.

[2] Pigou, *Economics of Welfare* [29], pp. 674 et seq. and Hicks [11], pp. 121 et seq.

has no *locus standi* when a "given quantity of capital" is conceived to be used for any number of different techniques, and embodied in any number of different outfits of capital goods.)

The conventional analysis, in terms of marginal products and the elasticity of substitution between factors, was, however, derived from considering a world in which the factors of production are labour and land. Land can be measured in physical units, and "quantities of factors" present then no more than the usual index-number difficulties which arise from differences in the natural qualities of different acres and of different men. Moreover, the notion of continuous variations in the proportions of factors employed with given knowledge seems less unplausible when we think of it as degrees of intensity of cultivation of the soil within the framework of an unchanging agricultural tradition. The marginal product of a given amount of labour is then the addition to output due to using one more man-year on a given space, and the marginal product of a given amount of land is the addition to output due to using one more acre with a given number of man-years of work. The elasticity of substitution is the ratio of a small proportionate change in the relative amounts of the factors employed to the proportionate change in the relative marginal productivities to which it gives rise.

When the "factors" in the conventional analysis are taken to be land and labour, each homogeneous within itself, there is no difficulty in reconciling our system of analysis with the conventional one, for an invention which, at the given prices of the factors, would cause an equal proportionate reduction in land and in labour per unit of output (that is, one which involves a neutral innovation in our sense), at given proportions of the factors would cause an equal proportionate rise in their marginal products. Such an innovation leaves the relative shares in proceeds of land and labour unchanged provided that the elasticity of substitution between them is equal to unity.[1]

I leave those who draw production functions to say what marginal productivity and the elasticity of substitution mean when labour and capital are the factors of production.

8. INVESTMENT OPPORTUNITIES

So far we have discussed the effect of innovations on the long-period supply-price of commodities. We must now glance at the short-period aspect of the problem, that is, at the influence of innovations on investment.

In the usual static analysis, an economy is treated as reaching equilibrium in "a given state of knowledge". An invention is then a "shock" to the system, and gives rise to investment in capital embodying a new technique of production. But in reality, of course, technical progress is continuous, and, moreover it is, in a certain sense, foreseen and allowed for. If a future innovation were foreseen in full detail it would begin to be made at once; innovations are foreseen by entrepreneurs in a vague way—they expect that there will be technical progress, each in his particular line, though they do not foresee exactly what form it will take. For this reason long-lived equipment is normally charged with an obsolescence allowance which is designed to write off its value before its physical life is fully exhausted. The reinvestment of amortisation funds in improved equipment is not in itself a "shock" giving rise to net investment.

[1] Further, whatever the elasticity of substitution, a neutral innovation leaves the relative shares unchanged if the elasticities of supply of the factors are equal. But it is hard to give any meaning to this condition except in the case where the elasticities of supply are zero. See [34].

Yet, at the same time, technical progress does give rise to investment opportunities. It does so by increasing the potential real income of the community.

Consider an economy in which technical progress is going on at a regular rate, to which the system has become accustomed, so that amortisation allowances are reckoned on the basis of the rate of obsolescence which is in fact being experienced. The whole stock of capital is being continuously done over as amortisation funds are re-invested in the latest kind of equipment. Then (provided that the proportion of consumption demand to real income is not decreasing excessively[1]) rising productivity creates investment opportunities by generating effective demand to take up the product of new capital.

The point is most clearly seen if we imagine an economy in which the income elasticity of demand for each particular type of consumption good is zero. The effects of each round of technical progress on national income can then be clearly seen, like the rings which mark the annual growth of a tree. In a certain period total consumption absorbs certain rates of output of commodities A to N. Now there is an increase in output per man-hour in producing these commodities and in providing the equipment required to produce them with new techniques. With a constant money-wage rate per hour, prices fall, and the purchasing power of a given money income over commodities A to N is increased, but no one wants any more of them. The public, however, is now ready to purchase commodity M, and provided that investment has meanwhile been made in equipment to produce M, both the labour released from producing A to N and the real effective demand released by the cheapening of A to N, is available to produce and to purchase M. And so on,

[1] See p. 32.

through time, to omega. In such a clearcut case we could see each successive rise in productive capacity manifested in a new commodity. In reality, of course, new commodities and increases in the quantities of old commodities consumed are inextricably tangled up, but the principle at work is the same as that which is seen in our imaginary case.

We must now consider the effect on investment of a change in the rate of technical progress. This divides into two questions: the consequences of having a higher rate of progress, to which the system is adjusted, and the consequences of an unforeseen change in the rate of progress.

The first question can be examined by the device of comparing two systems (each a closed world), each with expectations about the future moulded by its own past. In each entrepreneurs have become accustomed to expect the same, constant, rate of profit. Innovations, in each, are neutral on balance, and the ratio of the stock of capital to capacity output is the same in each. In each the proportion of saving to income is the same when "normal" income is being enjoyed, that is, when output is such as to keep equipment working at its normal capacity.

The only difference between the two systems is that in one, Alpha, the rate of technical progress is higher than in the other, Beta, so that, in each line of production, output per man-hour is rising faster in Alpha than in Beta.

Now, is there any reason to expect the rate of investment to be higher in Alpha than in Beta? Evidently not, for since the propensity to save (in real terms) is the same in each, the rate of accumulation of capital that can be steadily maintained is also the same.[1] The difference

[1] See p. 27 for a fuller discussion of this point.

between them shows itself in a more rapid rise in real wages per man-hour in Alpha, and a greater amount of technological unemployment, or a more rapidly falling number of hours worked per man-year, as the case may be. The effective length of life of equipment is shorter in Alpha, and the proportion of net to gross income consequently lower. If both communities were to go in for full-employment policies, Alpha would shoot rapidly ahead of Beta, but as each follows the path of its own habitual rate of growth, capital and income in each advance at the same proportional rate.

Now consider the effect of an unforeseen speeding up of technical progress above the accustomed rate. Innovators discover sooner than usual new methods of production which undersell the old, or new commodities which deflect purchasing power from the former channels of demand. This renders old plant unprofitable before the date of its expected demise. Either new, innovating, entrepreneurs drive the old ones out of business and, so to say, occupy the territory which they evacuate, or the old scrap their equipment and invest in new types. In either case investment rises above its former rate and a boom develops. This is true no matter whether the new techniques are capital using or capital saving. A new plant knocking an old one out of business requires investment even if it embodies less capital per unit of capacity than the one it displaces. The amount of investment required to do over the stock of capital is, however, likely to be greater, and therefore the boom larger and longer lived, the more capital per unit of capacity the new methods require.

In the converse case, innovations fail to come forward at the expected rate, old plant works longer than formerly and the reinvestment of amortisation funds falls off, so that slump conditions set in.

9. Changes in the Capital Ratio

We have seen that, so long as technical progress is neutral, and so long as obsolescence allowances are calculated appropriately to it, no net investment is required to adapt the stock of capital which caters for a given rate of output to new techniques. We must now consider a somewhat perplexing question. When innovations are of the type which we have called "favourable to capital", the ratio of capital to output, measured in terms of product (with a constant rate of profit) rises as a result of the change in technique. Do innovations of this kind require net investment to provide an increase in capital equipment to produce the old output? (In our simple example, is there net investment in the industries A to N as well as investment in creating industry M?) The answer is partly verbal and partly a matter of substance.

To pick a way through the quagmire of index-number problems which surrounds all such questions, let us consider the case where the physical capital required for a given output is unalterable and technical progress shows itself purely in rising output per man-hour, of commodities or of machines, each unchanged in nature.

Suppose that an innovation takes place which raises output per man-hour in the processes which use machines to make final output, the processes which produce machines remaining unaffected. Assuming competitive conditions, the price of commodities then falls relatively to the price of machines, and the value of machines in terms of product rises.

The existing stock of machines (producing the old rate of output) have to be replaced by new machines which are physically like the old ones but which cost more, in terms of product, than the old ones did. (The replacement of a machine requires the same number of man-hours of work as before, but the purchasing power of an hour's labour over commodities has risen.)

It is a verbal question whether we choose to attribute the difference between the cost of a new machine and of the old one which it replaces to net investment or to describe it as a rise in the ratio of gross to net output. But it is a matter of substance how the entrepreneurs responsible for producing the old rate of output behave in this situation. If their consumption, or disbursement of dividends, remains the same, in real terms, while the additional purchasing power of the workers engaged in replacing machines leads to an increase in effective demand for consumption goods, the consequences are the same as when the rate of net investment increases. If the entrepreneurs consider it necessary to increase their saving (in real terms) in order to provide for the increase in capital, then the total of demand is unaffected, though its composition is altered (if we choose to say that investment occurs, in this case we must say that it is accompanied by a corresponding increase in thriftiness). In the first case the fact that the innovation is of the type which we call "favourable to capital" means that it tends to promote a boom, in the second it does not.

Conversely, innovations unfavourable to capital reduce the amount of capital, measured in terms of product, required to produce a given rate of output, and adaptation to the new technique has an effect similar to disinvestment, unless entrepreneurs indulge in consumption out of their redundant amortisation funds.

Other types of innovation can be assimilated to the case where capital remains unchanged in physical form, by the device of measuring the value of capital in terms of output, though in all except the simplest case index-number difficulties make the analysis imprecise.

The reaction of entrepreneurs to an increase in the real value of the equipment required to produce the old rate of output must depend to some extent upon the magnitude of the change, and to some extent upon whether the individual entrepreneurs responsible for the old rate of output are carrying out the change or are being replaced by new firms. Suppose that the innovation consists of a scheme for mechanising a line of production formerly carried out with hand tools, and suppose that there is little or no economy in working capital to offset the increase in equipment, so that the cost of the capital goods required to produce a given rate of output with the new method is considerably greater than that of replacing the corresponding quantity of tools. The old entrepreneurs may be quite unable to find the resources required to make the change-over by cutting their consumption, so that they must either get new finance or give place to competitors who treat the market which they have invaded as a field for new investment like any other. The innovation then leads to investment not offset by savings earmarked to provide for it, and it tends to promote boom conditions. In the converse case (in which the innovations which take place are unfavourable to capital) the entrepreneurs have more freedom of manoeuvre, and their behaviour must be conceived to depend mainly upon the policy they choose to pursue.

A capital-favouring innovation which leads to investment in this way, creates a single "hump" of investment opportunities. Once the change has run its course and transmogrified the whole of the old stock of capital, the new capital may be supposed to settle down to earn its own replacement in the usual way, and there is no further call for investment of this kind unless the next bout of technical change which attacks the industry is also of a capital-favouring character. There is no particular presumption that one bout of capital-favouring innovations will be followed by another. Rather the reverse, for the increase in the value of capital per unit of output which has occurred is likely to suggest capital-saving innovations (for instance, the more machines there are in use the greater are the opportunities for improving the methods of production in the machine-making sectors of industry). Thus it seems that investment due to capital-favouring innovations (or disinvestment due to innovations unfavourable to capital) is likely to occur as an occasional episode rather than as a persistent tendency in the process of development.

10. DIFFERENCES IN THE CAPITAL RATIO

Our categories of innovations, "neutral", "capital using", "capital favouring", etc., are framed in terms of the *changes* in the proportions of labour and capital which they require. It is instructive to consider also the implications of *having* different ratios. To examine this point we may resort once more to the device of comparing two closed systems which are alike in every respect except one. Alpha and Beta, let us suppose, have equal rates of net output of final commodities, at the moment when we are comparing them, and exactly similar labour forces and similar general conditions in every respect except for the techniques which they know and are using. Alpha has a technique which requires a smaller quantity of capital goods (measured in terms of wage units) than that used in Beta. Each has the stock of capital appropriate, with its own techniques, to the given rate of output and the durability and age-composition of the stock of capital is the same in each case, so that the same proportion of the stock has to be renewed every year in each economy. Now, if the rate of profit on capital is the same in Alpha and Beta, then the workers in Alpha enjoy a larger total real income, for they receive a larger share in an identical total product. Alternatively, if the workers receive the same total income in each system, the rate of profit on capital is higher in Alpha than in Beta.

The number of man-hours worked per year is greater in Beta, for more labour is required to provide for replacement of capital.[1] Thus Alpha has either more unemployment or a shorter working week. (If we had taken equal amounts of employment in the two systems, instead of equal net outputs of final commodities, as the basis of the comparison, net income would have been smaller in Beta.)

If the ratio of net investment to net income is the same in both systems, Beta's income will fall progressively behind Alpha's, for it requires more investment in Beta than in Alpha to provide the equipment for a given increment in the rate of output. Alternatively, if capacity output is expanding at the same rate in the two systems, Beta must be saving and investing at a greater proportionate rate than Alpha. Beta, so to say, can keep pace with Alpha only by running faster.

Thus it appears that (apart from a greater tendency to technological unemployment) Alpha is in every way in a superior position to Beta. This may seem paradoxical, for we are accustomed to regard a community (with a given labour force) as being more wealthy the more capital it has.

[1] Unless the difference is solely in the speed of productive processes. If Alpha's advantage consists in a lower ratio of working capital to output (owing to faster production) with the same rate of output per man-hour at all stages, employment for a given rate of net output is the same in both economies.

But that is because we are accustomed to take technical knowledge as given. If we turn the proposition round the other way, it ceases to seem strange. Alpha is better off than Beta because it requires less capital to do the same job.

Finally, it is interesting to consider the influence of costs upon the direction of technical change. First, it may be supposed that a low ratio of costs to prices, that is, a high rate of net profit, due to monopolistic conditions and a weak bargaining position of workers, is in general inimical to progress, for entrepreneurs are less likely to exert themselves when profits are easily come by.

What of the influence of the rate of interest? With any given level of net profit, the lower is the rate of interest, the larger is the element of wages in normal cost, with any given technique in use. Therefore the lower is the rate of interest, the greater is the incentive to the individual entrepreneur to find labour-saving improvements. Conversely, a high rate of interest (and difficulty in procuring finance) encourages capital saving. These two effects are not symmetrical in their consequences, for (except in extreme Malthusian conditions) the supply of available labour is independent of the demand for it, while, in the long run, the supply of capital is not. Labour which becomes redundant to requirements as a result of an increase in output per head may fall into technological unemployment, but in favourable circumstances this is painlessly absorbed in increasing leisure, and, in any case, it forms a permanent reserve of productive capacity to meet any future expansion in effective demand that may occur. Capital which becomes redundant is disinvested and disappears from the scene. Thus, in a private enterprise economy, productive capacity flourishes where the rate of interest is low and real wage rates high, and degenerates where interest is high and wages low.

ACKNOWLEDGMENTS AND DISCLAIMERS

1. Marx

2. Marshall

3. Rosa Luxemburg

4. Contemporaries
    i. Kalecki
    ii. Harrod
    iii. The Acceleration Principle
    iv. General

ACKNOWLEDGMENTS AND
DISCLAIMERS

THE DERIVATION of the foregoing from Keynes is so obvious and so pervasive as to need no separate discussion. The following notes deal with some other sources on which I have drawn.

1. MARX

Three major elements in the foregoing argument are derived from Marx; the first is the method of using a numerical model of "expanded reproduction" as the tool of analysis; the second is the importance given to the influence of technique on the demand for labour; the third is the conception of unemployment due to a deficiency of capital or a "reserve army of labour". It may be of assistance to the reader if I point out what appears to me to be the relation of my argument to some other points in Marx's system.

Value.

The "Keynesian Revolution", which divides the General Theory as much from Marx as from Ricardo, was the adoption of the money-value of labour (the wage rate) in place of the labour-value of money as the unit of account. The labour-value of money is a purely mythical conception, for money has no cost of production. It is a social convention, comparable to an alphabet. True, it is an institution which has a certain cost of upkeep (just as an alphabet requires maintenance by school teachers). In this cost labour in gold mining plays a part. But even if every transaction involving money had to be made by passing gold from hand to hand, still the value of money would not depend upon the cost of mining. Each generation inherits a stock of gold from the past which is a "free gift" from history (to make a convenient medium of exchange a commodity must be highly durable, so that when it has been in use for some time, its stock is large relatively to its rate of production) and if the stock is inconveniently small, even an unsophisticated community soon finds ways to augment it with acceptable tokens. Money is a creation of society, and the most essential element in the purchasing power of money is its purchasing power over one's neighbours' time.

Marx took over from Ricardo the conception of the labour-value of money and added to the mystification by reckoning in terms of the labour-value of *value*. But when we reckon in terms of the money-value of labour the time-honoured conundrum: Where did *value* come from? vanishes and we are left confronting an actual question: How are money prices related to money wages, that is, how does the wage of labour in terms of commodities behave as capital accumulates? Marx assumed, at least in Volume I of *Capital*, that, by and large, real-wage rates tend to be constant, so that, as capitalism develops and output per man-hour rises, the gap between the real income of workers and of capitalists grows ever wider. At this time of day it appears a more plausible generalisation that real-wage rates tend to rise with productivity. But in any case the choice between these two hypotheses is a question of fact, not of metaphysics.

Capital.

The labour theory of value has another aspect. The assertion that it is only labour which produces value means that it is not correct to treat capital as a "factor of production". In these essays we have been using "capital" in a concrete sense, to mean the stock of equipment and work-in-progress the use of which enables labour to produce output, and which is in turn produced by labour with its own use. When the word is taken in this sense it seems rather a hair-splitting question to dispute whether capital is productive itself, or only assists labour to be productive. But certainly a great deal of confusion has flourished in economic theory as a result of treating labour and capital as symmetrical concepts.

When by capital we mean finance, it is clearly inappropriate to regard it as a factor of production, though a distribution of wealth favourable to enterprise, and ease of borrowing due to a well organised financial system and a favourable state of confidence, facilitate the development of productivity.

There is certainly a sense in which accumulation may be said to promote productivity, but saving cannot be treated as a factor of production symmetrical with labour (though it might be treated as symmetrical with the birth rate). The concept of capital as *waiting* is useful for propaganda rather than logical analysis.

Thus Marx's refusal to treat capital as a factor of production seems well founded. Whether it is right to regard natural resources in the same way is more dubious, though to do so may have been a helpful stage in the development of thought. In general, Marx very much played down the influence of geography upon human affairs. In this respect the balance was redressed by Rosa Luxemburg and where her treatment of the subject departs from his, she seems to me to have improved it.

The three ratios.[1]

Marx set out his argument in terms of *value*, that is, the labour-time "embodied" in commodities. But when

[1] This section has been revised for the 2nd Edition.

information is given in terms of technology and distribution, a unit of *value* is redundant. We can translate the *values* of outputs, inputs and stocks of means of production into terms of physical commodities and flows of payments in terms of wage-units.

The analytical system is built up by means of three ratios: the rate of exploitation, the rate of profit on capital and the organic composition of capital. Marx divides gross annual output of industry as a whole into: (1) constant capital used up and replaced—that is, raw materials entering into final output and wear and tear of plant, represented by the symbol c; (2) variable capital—that is, the annual wage bill, v; and (3) surplus, that is interest, rent and profits, s. But constant and variable capital have other meanings as well. Variable capital stands for that part of the value of work in progress which is made up of wages costs, and constant capital stands for the rest—that is, stocks of materials and fixed equipment. This division corresponds to the idea that capital laid out in employing labour enables the capitalist to acquire *surplus value*, while materials can yield only their own *value*. But it seems to be the result of confusing the wage bill with the wage fund which a capitalist must advance as part of his working capital.

In an economy which is a going concern, wage goods are part of the general flow of output and the means of production that they require are part of the general stock. There is no physical counterpart, for the economy as a whole, of the financial wage funds of individual capitalists. (Marx evidently got the idea from Ricardo, who thought of the agricultural wage fund as a stock of corn, retained in the barns after one year's harvest to be paid out as wages over the following year.) In industry, the amount of surplus a capitalist gets out of his workers is not related in any particular way to the amount of capital he has invested in a wages fund. For instance, workers normally advance one week's worth of wages fund to their employers, and they would be more, not less, exploited if they were paid at longer intervals, so reducing the amount of their employers' capital locked up. It is variable capital in its aspect as wages per annum that yields surplus. The rate of exploitation, then, is s/v, the ratio of surplus per annum to wages per annum, and s/(c + v), which Marx calls the rate of profit, is the ratio of surplus to cost of production.

From a formal point of view it is only another way of expressing the share of profit in net output, but it has a political meaning. It implies that the workers are paying too high a fee for the accumulation, maintenance and management of the stock of capital, and that there is a cheaper and better way of getting the job done than by allowing this share in the product to entrepreneurs and owners of wealth.

The rate of profit on capital means much the same in Marx's system as in any other. The meaning of the third ratio, the organic composition of capital, is not so easy to recognise and must be discussed at greater length.

Organic composition of capital is the ratio of constant to variable capital. In which sense should we take it? It sounds as though it referred to the division of the stock of capital into its two parts, but its essential meaning is the ratio of labour embodied in the stock of means of production ("dead labour") to current employment ("living labour"). If we write C for the stock, measured in labour time, then organic composition is $C/(s+v)$, for $s+v$ represents the hours of current labour time being performed. However, this still involves a stock-flow confusion. It

---

[1] *Capital* [27], volume III, chapter 13.

would be better to write K for the value of the stock at the ruling rate of profit and L for the employed labour force, so that organic composition is K/L.

But there is no point in wrangling with the symbols. We must try to find the meaning of organic composition which fits the central proposition.

A constant rate of exploitation means that the share of surplus in net output is constant. Now, in terms of our categories, when the rate of profit is constant, neutral innovations leave the share of capital constant, and what we have called capital-favouring innovations raise it. But if the rule is that the relative shares do not vary with the technique employed, then what we have called innovations favourable to capital (those which increase capital per unit of labour when capital is measured in wage units) reduce the rate of profit. Thus it makes sense of the central proposition if we identify rising organic composition with an increase in capital per unit of labour[1].

This seems quite straightforward as far as the formal analysis is concerned. The difficulty about the "law of falling profits" lies in postulating a constant share of capital in net output when capital per unit of labour is rising. Where the real wage rate is constant (as Marx usually assumed it to be) any type of innovation which is not heavily capital-using must raise the rate of profit.

2. MARSHALL

Marshall acknowledged with great candour that he was flummoxed by the problem of dynamic analysis. After discussing the problem of equilibrium with falling supply price he writes: "But such notions must be taken broadly. The attempt to make them precise over-reaches our

[1] Cf. *An Essay on Marxian Economics* [36], p. 42.

strength."[1] And again: "The unsatisfactory nature of these results is partly due to the imperfections of our analytical methods. . . . We should have made a great advance if we could represent the normal demand and supply price as functions both of the amount normally produced and of the time at which that amount became normal."[2]

His difficulty is clearly seen in the famous diagram in appendix H to the *Principles*, where he draws a branched supply curve showing that an increase in output reduces supply price by more than a decrease raises it. This, of course, is a totally illegitimate use of a plane diagram, and has caused generations of smart Alecs to mock.

What he was trying to say is fairly clear, and may perhaps be put as follows: If the demand for a commodity is such, in situation Alpha, that the rate of output is, has long been, and is expected to continue at the rate $M + \triangle M$ per week, costs will be lower than it is in situation Beta, with output equal to M. Now if a change were to occur in situation Beta such as to carry output to $M + \triangle M$, then, after a little time, costs would fall to the level found in situation Alpha. Whereas a change in situation Alpha which caused output to contract to M would not lead to a rise in cost to the level found in situation Beta, but to something lower.

There are other indications that Marshall habitually thought of a movement to the right along a supply curve (output increasing) as a movement forward through time[3]. This accounts for the extraordinary importance that he attached to what now seems a mere *curiosum*—

[1] *Principles* [25], p. 460.
[2] [25], Appendix H., p. 809.
[3] See Shove, "The Place of Marshall's *Principles* in the Development of Economic Theory" [44], *Economic Journal*, December 1942, p. 312.

economies of large-scale industry in competitive conditions[1]. The reason is that he somehow boiled the effect of technical progress going on through time into the movement down his supply curve.

The dilemma in which Marshall found himself between a static analysis and a dynamic picture of the world comes to the surface in the definition of normal profits. If a given rate of profit is the supply price of a given quantity of capital and enterprise, then supply is constant when profits are normal, and it requires super-normal profits to call forth an increase in the stock of capital. But if accumulation is normally going on, "normal profits" must mean the level of profits calling forth a normal rate of accumulation.[2] This conflict is nowhere resolved.

Marshall's plan was to deal with the prices of particular commodities in Volume I of the *Principles*, and to leave the problem of the general price level and the total of output for a later volume. At the end of Volume I he foreshadows the General Theory, and looks for the key to fluctuations in total output in the inducement to invest in fixed capital,[3] but when the ghost of his projected treatment of the subject finally appeared as *Money, Credit and Commerce*, the General Theory was still to write.

What provisional assumptions he was meanwhile making about the behaviour of output as a whole cannot be said, and any view of what Marshall *really meant* can always be countered by quotations from the *Principles* which show conclusively that he meant just the opposite. All the same it may be worth while to try to find assump-

---

[1] Cf. Sraffa, " The Laws of Returns under Competitive Conditions " [45], *Economic Journal*, December 1926.

[2] Cf. Shove, " Mrs. Robinson on Marxian Economics " [43], *Economic Journal*, April 1944, p. 60.

[3] [25], p. 710–11.

tions that fit what seem to be the main dynamical elements in Marshall's scheme of ideas.

We found a deep-seated inconsistency in the conception of full employment preserved by movements in the rate of interest.[1] This objection can be met by postulating conditions in which the rate of interest does not need to vary appreciably in order to ensure full employment.

Imagine an economy in which there is no bottleneck of equipment or specialised skill in the capital-goods industries to limit the possible rate of investment. (This would be found if investment consisted mainly in appropriating hitherto unused natural resources such as timber, with the aid only of simple tools, as in Marshall's archetypal example of investment—a peasant building himself a weather-proof hut.[2]) Nor does finance set a limit. Any entrepreneur can borrow as much as he pleases at the ruling rate of interest. Ordinary labour is the only bottleneck.

As in our golden age, the rate of profit expected on new capital in the future is equal to the rate ruling in the present. So long as the rate of interest does not exceed the rate of profit, there is an indefinitely large increase in the stock of capital which entrepreneurs would like to make. The situation differs from our model in that the rate at which investment plans can be carried out is limited solely by the availability of labour. The amount of labour available for investment is the total *minus* that employed in consumption-goods industries. We must suppose that when normal prices prevail there are sufficient frictions to prevent workers employed in consumption-goods industries from being enticed away by investment-goods entrepreneurs, otherwise the situation would be

----

[1] See above, p. 10.   [2] *Principles* [25], p. 233.

chronically unstable.[1] But the investment-goods industries readily take on any workers who happen to come into the labour market. Thus full employment always prevails. Capital accumulates at the rate dictated by the full-employment rate of investment, and since investment always fills whatever gap there may be between consumption and full-employment output, there is never any problem of a deficiency of effective demand. (But here the unresolved conflict between static and dynamic theory leaves a hazy patch in the analysis.)

On these assumptions the demand for labour at any moment is perfectly elastic to the rate of interest, at the value of the rate of interest which coincides with the (actual and expected) rate of profit. For, if the rate of interest chanced to fall below this level, the price of existing capital goods would rise above the cost of production of new ones, excess demand in the capital-goods industries would break through the frictions in the labour market and an inflationary rise in wages and prices would set in. Conversely, if the rate of interest chanced to rise, new investment plans would cease to be made, the rate of investment would rapidly decline, and unemployment would occur. But in the first case, a rise in demand for money due to the rise in wages would quickly drive the rate of interest up, and, in the second, a fall in demand for money due to the fall in employment would quickly drive it down, so that it could not remain, for more than a passing flutter, at any level except that corresponding to the rate of profit.

(Our objection to a system in which the rate of interest regulates employment does not apply in this case, for the full-employment value of the rate of interest and the value normally experienced coincide.)

[1] Cf. above, p. 64.

The above seems to fit Marshall's view that the normal long-run level of the rate of interest is determined by the profitability of capital, and that any monetary disturbance which causes the market rate of interest to depart from this normal level generates a cumulative movement of prices which brings the market rate of interest back to equality with the rate of profit.[1]

There is an important element in common between this conception of a full-employment economy and our imagined golden age. In both the continuance of accumulation requires faith. Everything depends upon entrepreneurs acting on the belief that the present rate of profit will continue to be obtainable in the future. This is in accordance with Marshall's conception that slumps are caused by a failure of confidence and recoveries by its rebirth.[2]

The main difference between our model and this system of ideas arises from the central point of the General Theory. In our model a rise in thrift above the level to which the system is adjusted plunges the economy into a slump. In this one, an increase in thrift releases labour which is immediately used to speed up the rate at which investment plans are carried out, and from the point of view of effective demand the distinction between consumption and saving is of no importance. This fits Marshall's "familiar economic axiom that a man purchases labour and commodities with that portion of his income which he saves just as much as with that which he is said to spend."[3]

There is one part of Marshall's system which does not

---

[1] See " Evidence before the Committee on Indian Currency " [24], *Official Papers*, p. 274. Cf. Wicksell, *Interest and Prices* [48], p. 95.

[2] *Principles* [25], p. 711.

[3] *Pure Theory of Domestic Values* [26], p. 34.

fit into this interpretation: that is the conception of the rate of interest as the supply price of "waiting". "The supply price of waiting" must surely mean the rate of interest at which owners of wealth are just willing to refrain from consuming their capital in "present gratifications", that is, the rate of interest at which there would be zero net saving.[1] For accumulation to be taking place, the rate of profit, and therefore the rate of interest, must be above this level. The zero-saving rate of interest may well be negative—if there were no other way to carry wealth from the present to the future its owners would be willing to pay safe-deposit keepers to mind it for them. Thus a great part, or more than the whole, of what the owners of wealth receive for the service of "waiting" is a pure economic rent.

The notion that interest measures the "real cost" of the "sacrifices" of owning wealth belongs to the static layer in Marshall's thought and makes no sense when it is transplanted into a dynamic setting.

3. ROSA LUXEMBURG

Rosa Luxemburg[2] constructs a model of a capitalist economy in which the following conditions prevail: Real-wage rates are held down at a constant level. There is a plentiful reserve army of labour, the unemployed sharing the wages of the employed so that their existence adds nothing to effective demand. As technical progress increases productivity, the share of labour in national income falls. The sole passion of capitalists is to save and accumulate, so that, as their share in total income rises, the

---

[1] Mr. Shove [43] challenged this view, but his argument on this point is excessively obscure.

[2] *The Accumulation of Capital* [23].

proportion of saving to total income rises still faster. The system therefore cannot follow the path of steady accumulation shown in our model, of which an essential characteristic is that the proportion of income saved is constant.

Rosa Luxemburg rejects Tugan Baranowski's suggestion that capital-using technical progress could absorb the rising proportion of saving. She therefore has to find some other way to account for the fact that accumulation can occur.

It is clear that *if* the capitalists each week invest the savings of the week before and employ labour to operate the capital so created, accumulation can go on indefinitely. But the increase in demand for consumption goods each week is less than the increase in potential output due to last week's increment to the stock of capital. How then are the capitalists induced to maintain investment?[1]

Her solution is as follows: The capitalist nations are surrounded by primitive economies, each insulated from the others like a nut within its shell, waiting to be cracked. The capitalists break open a primitive economy and enter into trade with it, whether by enticing its inhabitants with commodities they have never seen before, by political cunning or by brute force. Now exports to the primitives provide an outlet for the product of the last batch of capital goods created at home. After a little while another nut is broken, a use for more capital is thereby found, and so on, as long as the supply of untouched primitive economies lasts. Thus each year's exports are larger than those of the year before, and investment in enlarging the stock of capital can continue.

There is no need to ask why an individual capitalist should export, or, so long as exports are expanding, why

---

[1] [23], p. 131 et seq.

he invests, for each is thinking only of finding a market for his goods. But it is necessary to inquire how the system keeps in balance. Each year exports are larger than the year before and the income of the capitalist economy is greater. Each year more workers are employed at home and the total of consumption out of wages increases. So does consumption out of profits, for the capitalists do not save the whole increment of their incomes. The increase in consumption provides a demand for imports to match the growing exports, so that trade may remain balanced, and there is not necessarily any export of capital. But the capitalists' consumption at most increases in proportion to their incomes (and normally increases by less) and their share in total income is rising. The ratio of saving to income each year is greater than the year before. Investment must therefore be greater each year, and to keep the growing stock of capital employed, the increment of exports must be greater each year. Thus a larger nut must be broken each time than the time before, and capitalist trade must spread in an ever-widening circle. When the stock of unbroken nuts is exhausted, the capitalist system collapses for want of markets.

This is Rosa Luxemburg's theory in its pure form.[1] It is supplemented by the more obvious argument that in the course of their conquests the capitalists find stores of natural resources and facilities for production in the territories of the primitives, and in these they find large opportunities for new capital projects, so that exports exceed imports for long periods while foreign investment is going on. One of the main attractions is the means to produce exotic' commodities which cannot be grown at home. The capital goods set up abroad and the territories

[1] This interpretation is defended in the introduction to the English edition of *The Accumulation of Capital* [23].

and mineral deposits appropriated, by fair means and foul, from the primitives, provide raw materials for the industries at home and food for the increasing number of workers employed.

On this view, Rosa Luxemburg's theory in no way resembles the various kinds of nonsense that have been attributed to her, though it must be admitted that there are a number of confusions and obscurities in her exposition of it.

4. CONTEMPORARIES

I. KALECKI

Mr. Kalecki's discovery of the General Theory independently of Keynes was a classic example of the coincidences of science. His version of the analysis led directly (which Keynes' did not) to a model of the trade cycle. Based upon the same conception of short-period equilibrium, his theory fitted naturally into Keynes' scheme, and became absorbed into it in the subsequent development of the General Theory. By now it is impossible to distinguish what one has learned from which.

I am chiefly conscious of a debt to Mr. Kalecki for his way of handling expectations as an average of past experience—a simple device which enables us to conceive of beliefs about the future which are going to be proved correct (in stable conditions) without being obliged to deprive those who hold them of Free Will.

My chief difference from Mr. Kalecki is in respect of his treatment of finance as the short-period bottleneck.

II. HARROD

I have profited very greatly from Mr. Harrod's

Towards a Dynamic Economics[1]—indeed the central point of the foregoing analysis is taken from it—and I have been much impressed by the subtlety of his theoretical analysis. All the same I totally disagree with his application of it.

Mr. Harrod sets out his argument in terms of what he calls the "natural rate of growth". The "natural" rate is that which would be realised with continuous full employment and a rate of technical progress which is regarded as arbitrary (not to be speeded up or slowed down by economic influences). It would be more perspicuous to call this the *maximum feasible* rate of growth. This rate of growth of output requires a certain rate of growth in the stock of capital.

The "warranted rate of growth" is of the same form as the steady rate of growth depicted in our model. The key ratio in it is the proportion of income saved. This (in combination with the ratio of capital to output) indicates the rate of accumulation of capital that is "warranted" by the thriftiness of the economy.

Mr. Harrod compares the rate of accumulation appropriate to the maximum feasible rate of growth with that shown by the warranted rate. He regards the situation in which the warranted rate is the greater of the two as the most likely to be found in reality, and proposes remedies to deal with the problem to which this gives rise.[2]

Now the situation of a maximum feasible rate of growth

---

[1] Professor E. D. Domar (" Expansion and Employment " [2], *American Economic Review*, March 1947) sets out, independently of Mr. Harrod, what is essentially the same model of steady accumulation, but he does not deal with the relations between full-capacity working of capital and full employment of labour.

[2] Mr. T. C. Schelling (" Capital Growth and Equilibrium " [40], *American Economic Review*, December 1947) criticises the " warranted rate of growth " conceived as a state of equilibrium. His objections to any

less than the warranted rate is one in which thriftness is excessive, not merely in relation to the investment which profit-seeking entrepreneurs are willing to make, but in relation to the rate of accumulation of capital which is useful to society. This is the dynamical equivalent of Bliss.[1]

Bliss, in its static aspect, is a situation in which, with given, unchanging tastes and technical knowledge, natural resources and population, the accumulation of capital has been carried to the point where there is no use for any more capital (not even more pyramids). Any increment to the stock of capital made after Bliss has been achieved would just be a nuisance and would have to be cleared away again.

In its dynamical aspect, the stock of capital for which a use can be found is not constant, but increases with population and technical knowledge. The situation contemplated by Mr. Harrod is one where the thriftiness of the community is capable of providing for a rate of accumulation greater than this, even after the rate of interest has been brought as low as possible.

A community whose only problem was that they have all the capital that there is any use for, would not really have a great deal to worry about, and we need not wring our hearts by contemplating their troubles.

III. THE ACCELERATION PRINCIPLE

It may be useful to discuss the relationship of the fore-

such notion are supported by the analysis of the foregoing essay, but his interpretation of what Mr. Harrod intended is dubious, for Mr. Harrod's main point is that the warranted rate cannot normally be achieved in pure *laisser faire* conditions.

[1] Keynes, *Treatise* [22], p. 163. The reference to Frank Ramsey's article in the *Economic Journal* is wrongly given. It should be December 1928.

going analysis to the "acceleration principle". According to this principle an increase in income "induces" investment, whereas, according to the foregoing analysis, it is an increase in the stock of capital (combined with a corresponding increase in utilised natural resources, improved technique and, where required, an increase in the employed population) which makes an increase in income possible.

The notion of "induced" investment is fully applicable to working capital. The decision by an entrepreneur to increase the rate of output of a commodity involves in itself a decision to invest in working capital. Moreover, the timing of the investment is determined by the same decision. While output is in the course of expanding, the value of work in progress grows at a rate determined by technical conditions, and when output has reached its new level, investment ceases. This can quite simply be described as investment induced by an increase in output. But when we consider long-lived productive equipment (ships, machines, factory buildings) the notion becomes vague and unseizable. Suppose that an entrepreneur has recently experienced a ten per cent increase in the weekly demand for the commodity he produces. Before we know anything about what investment this will induce we must ask: (1) How near to capacity was he working his plant before the increase in demand occurred? (2) For how many weeks does he expect the new rate of demand to last? From the answers to these questions we can deduce what change (if any) in his capital equipment he is likely to want to make. There is no particular presumption that it will be ten per cent. But, even if it happened to be so, the question would still remain: Over what period of time will the investment be made, which will add ten per cent to his stock of capital? On this the acceleration principle does not throw the faintest ray of light. The difficulty is still greater when we consider a fall in demand. The decision to reduce the rate of output of a commodity involves in itself a decision to disinvest in working capital, but what amount, and what rate, of disinvestment in equipment is induced by a given fall in demand?[1]

Mr. Hicks, in his *Contribution to the Theory of the Trade Cycle*, attempting to meet these objections, sophisticates the acceleration principle out of all recognition.

Professor Samuelson, on the other hand, following, as Marshall would say, his mathematics boldly, makes the rate of investment a function of the rate of change of income, without even distinguishing an upswing which follows the path of a recent boom, and finds capacity waiting to meet it, from one which exceeds any previous output and has all its equipment to make[2].

The distinction between the acceleration principle and the method of argument used in the foregoing essay disappears when we are concerned with continuous steady development. If steady progress has been going on ever since Adam left Paradise so that the stock of capital is fully adjusted to current demand at every moment in history, the distinction between working and fixed capital does not arise, and it does not make any difference whether we regard investment as induced by the increase in output or as resulting from the relation between current demand and the stock of capital available to cater for it. Thus there is no conflict between Mr. Harrod's "warranted rate of growth" and our model of steady progress, in spite of the fact that Mr. Harrod

[1] Cf. Tinbergen, *The Dynamics of Business Cycles* [47], p. 164 et seq. Hahn, "A Recent Contribution to Trade Cycle Theory" [7], *Quarterly Review, Banca Nazionale del Lavoro*, December 1950.

[2] Samuelson, *Foundations of Economic Analysis* [38], p. 341.

formulates his conception in terms of the acceleration principle. But when we are concerned with an economy which is off the steady path, the acceleration principle becomes a great impediment to clear thinking.

IV. GENERAL

There are a great number of contemporary authors to whom I am indebted for particular points, and so I fear that I may not have mentioned all of them where I should. Ever since the *Treatise on Money* was published there has been a great proliferation of dynamic theorising, and one is picking up so many ideas all the time (sometimes one's own returned with knobs on) that it is hard to keep track of their sources. I should like to make here a general apology for all errors and omissions that I have committed.

THE RATE OF INTEREST

THE RATE OF INTEREST

THE PROBLEM to be discussed is the determination of the rate of interest in a closed economy, working under *laisser faire* in the sense that the authorities use no means to influence conditions except monetary policy.

The question is to some extent imaginary because in the days when *laisser faire* ruled an important influence on the rate of interest in any one country was the state of its balance of payments, and the objective of momentary policy was control of the foreign exchanges. When the break-up of the world capital market, and exchange control, have largely insulated interest rates in each country there is no longer *laisser faire* in other respects. However, our problem is sufficiently complicated to justify drastic simplification.

I. INTRODUCTION

The most important influences upon interest rates—which account for, say, the difference between 30% in an Indian village and 3% in London—are social, legal, and institutional. Side by side with the industrial revolution went great technical progress in the provision of credit and the reduction of lender's risk and great changes in social habits favourable to lending; and in the broad sweep of history these considerations are more significant than any others. But we are here concerned with an economy in which the most up-to-date credit facilities may be taken for granted and a capitalist system is fully developed.

First let us consider the influence upon interest rates of the "fundamental phenomena of Productivity and Thrift".[1] It is generally agreed that a fall in interest rates tends to stimulate investment and that a low rate of interest is more likely to discourage than to encourage saving. In any given situation, then, we may say that there is some value of the rate of interest so low as to lead to full employment (but at times this rate may be negative). The full-employment rate is strongly influenced by the "real force" of thrift and, if not by the "real force" of productivity, at least by beliefs about the future profitability of capital, which is related to it. In a *laisser faire* competitive economy, with free wage-bargaining, if the full-employment rate were ever above the actual rate, inflation would set in through a rise of money-wage rates and the rate of interest would be driven up.[2] The full-employment value of the rate of interest may therefore be regarded as, in a certain sense, a lower limit to the possible value of the rate of interest. If this limit always lies far below any value of the actual rate of interest ever experienced, it has little influence on the actual rate. But if from time to time the "real forces" sweep the full-employment rate above the actual rate, and force the actual rate up (whether by causing inflation or by inducing the monetary authorities to raise the actual rate in order to avoid inflation), then clearly they do play a part in determining the course of the actual rate.[3]

---

[1] Robertson, *Essays in Monetary Theory* [32], p. 25.

[2] Cf. above, p. 63.

[3] The theory that, if money wages are sufficiently variable, the rate of interest automatically tends to its full-employment value is discussed above, pp. 7 et seq. Even when this theory can be made to seem plausible on its own ground, it has no application here, for it belongs to long-period static theory, while the purpose of this paper is to sketch a theory of interest which might be useful in historical analysis.

Moreover, an important influence upon the actual rate, at any moment, are expectations of the future course of interest rates, and expectations are strongly influenced by the historical experience of interest rates which the community has lived through. If the real forces play some part in shaping that historical experience, they have some influence upon the position of the rate of interest even when the full-employment rate, at the moment, is far below it. Thus the real forces have a roundabout influence on the actual rate of interest, as well as upon the full-employment rate. There is then, after all, a Cheshire cat to grin at Professor Robertson,[1] but it often happens that the grin, cheerful or sour, remains after the circumstances which give rise to it in the past have completely vanished from the present scene.

2. THE STRUCTURE OF THE MARKET

Let us turn to the monetary forces acting on the rate of interest. Keynes' theory treated the rate of interest as determined by the demand and supply of money. This was a useful simplification in the pioneering days of the theory, but it was always obvious that there is no such thing as *the* rate of interest and that the demand and supply of every type of asset has just as much right to be considered as the demand and supply of money.

To develop a more refined theory the notion of liquidity preference, measured by the reward required to induce owners of wealth to hold assets other than money, must be broken up into a number of aspects. Among the disadvantages of various kinds of assets compared to money we may distinguish:

[1] [32], p. 25.

1. Illiquidity in the narrow sense. Liquidity partly consists in the capacity of an asset to be realised in money. A limited and imperfect market, the cost and trouble of making a sale, and the time required to effect it, reduce the liquidity of an asset quite apart from variability in its price. Liquidity in the narrow sense depends upon the power to realise its value in cash, whatever the value may be at the moment. To avoid confusion with Keynes' language we will call this quality "convenience" instead of "liquidity".

2. Uncertainty of future capital value, or capital-uncertainty for short, due not to any fear of failure by the borrower but to the possibility of changes in capital values owing to changes in the ruling rate of interest. (This is the main ingredient in Keynes' conception of liquidity preference. He regards the rate of interest primarily as a premium against the possible loss of capital if an asset has to be realised before its redemption date.)

3. Lender's risk, that is, the fear of partial or total failure of the borrower.

Further, when comparing long-term bonds with other paper assets we have to add one more factor:

4. Uncertainty as to the income that a sum of money now committed to the asset will yield in the future, or income-uncertainty for short.

These qualities make up the character, or, so to say, natural colour, of various types of assets. (The relationship of present to expected prices is a separate element in the complex of influences governing the demand for the various assets at any moment.)

A modern capital market represents a bewildering variety of assets, with these qualities in all sorts of.

combinations. To make our inquiry manageable we must draw a simplified and stylised picture of the market, selecting only a few sharply defined types of assets, say three months' bills, irredeemable bonds, and ordinary shares.[1] We will further simplify by assuming that owners of wealth hold only money or paper assets, while real assets are owned by entrepreneurs who hold them against borrowed funds;[2] that money consists only of bank deposits, without distinction between current and deposit accounts; and that the quantity of money is rigidly determined by the basis of credit which the Central Bank chooses to provide, as in the ideal text-book picture of the British banking system.[3]

[1] The distinction between shares and loans raises some legal and philosophical problems. At one point in the *General Theory* [21], chapter XII, Keynes creates confusion by calling ordinary shares "real assets", and describing a purchase of shares on the Stock Exchange as an act of investment. It seems both simpler and less unrealistic to go to the opposite extreme, treating shares as a type of paper asset like the rest and regarding their yield as one of the rates of interest. This is, in essence, the way that those in charge of real investment decisions probably most often look at the matter; to the managing director of a joint-stock company there is a great deal in common between a share-holder and a creditor. The conception of yield also presents some complications. It may be calculated on the basis of earnings or of dividends, and on the basis of expected future returns or past realised returns. We shall not enter into these difficulties in the present discussion, but in general we are concerned with prospective yield.

[2] An entrepreneur operating real capital which he owns is regarded as *pro tanto* an owner of wealth lending to himself. Cf. Modigliani, "Liquidity Preference and the Theory of Interest" [28], p. 30. Where a citizen lives in his own house, we may regard him as an owner of wealth lending to himself as an entrepreneur who sells to himself as a consumer.

When there is doubt about the future purchasing power of money, owners of wealth become entrepreneurs; that is to say, there is "flight into real values". The whole question of liquidity then takes on quite a different aspect, and money ceases to be the asset to which liquidity preference attaches. We shall not concern ourselves with this problem, but assume that we are discussing a community which has confidence in the future purchasing power of its money.

[3] The argument can easily be modified to fit the case where the supply of money has some elasticity and responds to changes in the rate of interest which the banks can earn.

Bills we will assume to be perfectly "good" in the sense that they are free of lender's risk, and they are so short-dated that capital-uncertainty is very small.[1] Bills then differ from money in little except their inferior "convenience". Our bonds, we may suppose, also are perfectly good, and no less "convenient" than bills, in the sense that they can be readily marketed at any time (or pledged against a loan).

The difference between them arises from uncertainty. In a world where past experience has been that interest rates vary from time to time there is uncertainty about future interest rates, in the sense that, whatever an individual may believe about the most probable future course of interest rates, he does not hold his belief with perfect conviction. An owner of wealth who buys a bill today knows what his capital will be in three months' time, but he is uncertain what interest he will then be able to get by re-investing it.[2] If he buys a bond, he knows his income for as long as he likes to hold the bond, but he is uncertain about what his capital will be worth at any date in the future. Perfectly good bills thus offer negligible capital-uncertainty, but relatively high income-uncertainty, while perfectly good bonds offer perfect certainty of income, but relatively high capital-uncertainty.

---

[1] But see below, p. 150.

[2] It is uncertainty about the whole complex of interest rates that is relevant, not expectations about the bill rate only. Mr. Kalecki (*Studies in Economic Dynamics* [17], p. 37) takes as typical the case of a person comparing the result of "holding one or the other type of security over a few years"—that is, choosing between buying a bond now and deciding now not to buy a bond for a few years, holding bills during that time. But usually an owner of wealth feels himself free to switch his capital from one asset to another at any time in the future if it seems good to him. Mr. Kaldor "Speculation and Economic Stability" [15], *Review of Economic Studies*, October 1939, p. 13, uses a similar argument, which is subject to the same objection.

Shares are subject to income-uncertainty of a special kind because of uncertainty about the future profits to be earned by the real assets to which they correspond. They are therefore subject to a double dose of capital-uncertainty, for their prices vary both with changes in profit-expectations and with changes in the rates of interest. Moreover, they are subject to lender's risk, in varying degrees, according to the standing and reputation of the firms which they represent.

These qualities of the various types of asset are differently evaluated by different individuals. Some (widows and orphans) set great store on income-certainty, and do not bother much about capital-uncertainty, as they do not intend to realise in any case. Financial institutions set great store on their balance sheets, and value capital-certainty very highly. Owners of wealth with a taste for speculation, or those who have such a large fortune that they can spread their risks widely, have a smaller aversion than either to uncertainty about any particular asset. The general pattern of interest rates depends upon the distribution of wealth between owners with different tastes, relatively to the supplies of the various kinds of assets.

Each type of asset is a potential alternative to every other; each has, so to speak, a common frontier with every other, and with money. Equilibrium in the market is attained when the interest rates are such that no wealth is moving across any frontier. Prices are then such that the market is content to hold just that quantity of each type of asset which is available at the moment.

The complex of demands and supplies is not static, but is moving slowly through time. Over any period there is an increment to total wealth from saving equal to the borrowing for investment (and budget deficits) that has taken place during the period. The total of wealth, representing a demand for paper assets, increases with the supply. But the supply of any particular type may alter relatively to the demand for it. For instance, a budget deficit, financed by selling bonds, will generate savings which the owners wish to put partly into money or shares. The supply of bonds is then increasing relatively to demand.

A borrower who is free to choose the kind of paper assets he creates will try to offer those which require the lowest interest, and this sets up a certain tendency for supply gradually to be adjusted to demand (though changes in business methods—the growth of self-financing, the decay of the trade bill—may alter supply in a way quite unrelated to changes in demand).

There is also a much more immediate way in which supply is adjusted to demand. Where there is a difference between interest rates there is a possible source of profit. If the short rate were found on the average to rule above the long, because of the dominance in the market of widows and orphans with a strong preference for bonds, and if this situation were expected to continue, financial houses could issue bonds, which would be taken up by the widows and orphans, and use the funds thus obtained to carry bills. They would undergo a risk, for if there were an unforeseen change, and the short rate fell permanently, they could only get out of the now unprofitable business by redeeming their bonds, which might meanwhile have risen in price. Thus the long rate would still have to remain normally lower than the short rate.

In the reverse case (which is the usual one, at least in recent times) where preference for capital-certainty predominates in the market, so that the bond rate exceeds the bill rate, there is an income to be made by borrowing short and lending long. This is commonly done by taking a bank advance. Assuming the basis of credit to remain constant, the banks must sell other assets when they increase advances, and their assets are short-dated (in our simplified world they could only hold bills) so that the effect is the same as though dealers in credit issued bills in order to hold bonds. The risk involved in this operation is that there may be an unforeseen rise in the bill rate, so that the dealers have either to renew their loans at a higher cost or to sell out bonds whose price may have fallen. Thus these operations require a margin between long and short term rates and, since there is not an un-limited amount of credit available to dealers, the margin they require will be larger the greater the amount of bonds that they are holding.

Investment trusts issue what are intended to be less speculative securities in order to carry more speculative ones.

Operations such as these to some extent smooth out the differences in demand for securities of different types and bring the various interest rates closer together.

3. Changes in the Quantity of Money and in Expectations

Preferences for various types of asset, relatively to the supplies of them, determine the general pattern of interest rates, and it is against this sort of background that day-to-day changes in interest rates occur. The pattern most commonly found in actual markets is such that normally the bill rate is lower than the bond rate, and the yields of shares higher.

Given the general background, there are two quite distinct types of influence which play upon the equili-brium pattern of rates. One is the state of expectations and the other is the supply of money. To discuss them separately we require to be able to assume one constant when the other varies. It is difficult to frame the assumption that expectations are given without sawing off the bough we are sitting on. It is easiest to discuss expectations if they are quite definite. Everything can then be reduced to arithmetic. But if we assume that owners of wealth have clear and unanimous expectations about the exact future course of the prices of assets, in which they believe with perfect confidence, then we have ruled out uncertainty and stepped into a world quite unlike the one we want to discuss. Moreover, we have landed ourselves in a logical impasse, for either the expectations will turn out to be correct, in which case there is no more to be said, or they will turn out mistaken, in which case perfect confidence cannot persist.

The whole subject of expectations bristles with psychological and philosophical difficulties,[1] and I can offer only a sketchy and superficial treatment of it. For the moment let us be content to assume that the bond rate is expected to move around the average level that has been experienced in the recent past, so that when it falls below that level it is expected to rise, some time or other, and when it rises above, to fall, but that everyone's view is hazy as to how long it will take to return to the average value and how far it will go meanwhile, so that there is great uncertainty about what its value will be at any particular date in the future. For simplicity of exposition we will suppose that we are examining the market at a moment when today's bond rate is equal to the average value. Further, we will assume that profits are expected to continue at the same level as in the recent past, so that the prices of shares are not expected to move except in

[1] Cf. Shackle, *Expectation in Economics* [42], especially chapter VII, and Fellner, *Monetary Policies and Full Employment* [5], pp. 152 et seq.

response to changes in the rate of interest. Finally, we will neglect speculators operating on day-to-day changes in the price of assets.

Having thus tethered expectations, let us examine the effect upon the market of a change in the quantity of money. A change in the amount of bank deposits is a special case of the kind of change in the stock of assets relative to the total of wealth which we have already discussed.[1] The essence of the matter is that when the Central Bank, say, increases the basis of credit the member banks buy assets from the market to an amount which restores the normal ratio of their cash reserves to other assets. They thus reduce the amount of assets to be held by the market and so raise their prices. To maintain our simplifying assumptions we will assume that the banks buy only bills. The immediate consequence is a fall in the rate of interest on bills. What effect does this have upon the bond rate?

The bond rate is bound to be affected, for even if all owners of wealth have strong preferences, and are settled far from the frontier between bonds and bills, so that it would need a very large change in values to shift them, yet dealers in credit will react to small changes and so provide a continuously sensitive frontier between bills and bonds. The profit to be made by selling a bill and buying a bond is the difference in the interest on them for three months *minus* the fall (or *plus* the rise) in the price of the bond over three months. Dealing at today's prices, the difference in interest which will be enjoyed is known, but the change in price of the bond is unknown. A fall in the short rate increases the difference in interest rates, and so raises the demand for bonds, but the consequent rise in the price of bonds enhances the likelihood of a fall

[1] See p. 144.

in their price in the future. If expectations are clear and definite, only a very small fall in the long-term rate of interest can occur. It needs a fall of only $\frac{1}{4}\%$ in the price of bonds over three months to wipe out the effect of a fall of 1% in the bill rate per annum, and a rise in today's price of bonds by $\frac{1}{4}\%$ means a fall in the bond rate of interest in the ratio 400:401.[1] Suppose, for example, that there is a clear expectation that the bond rate will be back to its average in three months' time; then today's rate cannot fall by more than this ratio in response to each 1% fall in the bill rate.[2] But if expectations of what the bond rate will be in three months' time are vague and dubious, the power of a rise in today's price of bonds to wipe out the attraction of holding them is so much the weaker. Thus the effect of a fall in the short rate upon the long is greater, the greater the uncertainty in which the market dwells.

In the *Treatise on Money*, Keynes, so to speak, dramatised uncertainty as the existence of "two views" leading to a "bull-bear position"—that is, a dispersion of opinions, each confidently held.[3] The degree of uncertainty in the market as a whole then depends on the variety of opinion within it. The same effects follow where everyone is alike, but no one feels confident that his own best guess of what the future holds will turn out to be right. In any situation where there is inadequate evidence on which to base predictions, both elements will be present. Thus a rise in today's price of bonds will induce some holders of bonds

[1] Cf. *General Theory* [21], p. 168.

[2] This relationship is quite sufficient to account for the observed sluggishness in the movement of the long-term rate of interest in response to changes in the short rate. It is unnecessary as well as unplausible to maintain that the long rate responds only to changes in the *expected future* short rate. Cf. above, p. 142, note 2.

[3] In the *Treatise* [22], chapter XV the two views refer to future share prices, but Keynes applies the same idea to views about the rate of interest (*General Theory* [21], pp. 169 and 173).

to sell before others, and will cause many holders to sell out to some extent. The greater the dispersion of opinion and the less confidently are opinions held, the greater the movement of bond prices in response to a given change in the quantity of money.

We have assumed that expectations of profit are constant. With lower interest rates the frontiers between bills and shares and bonds and shares are no longer in equilibrium at the old rate, and there is a sympathetic movement in the price of shares, governed by similar considerations to those which influence the movement of bond prices. Thus an increase in the quantity of money lowers the whole complex of interest rates.

We may now look at the same situation the other way up and inquire what has happened to the increment of money which has been created. At any moment some money is in course of travelling round the active circulation—from income earner to shopkeeper, from shopkeeper to producer, from producer to income earner, and so back again. Some is in the financial circuit, passing between buyers and sellers of paper assets. Some is lodged in what we may call a "short hoard" either because its owner, who has recently made some savings, is shortly going to spend it in buying securities, or because its owner (who may be an entrepreneur) has some large-scale purchase of goods shortly to make. These short hoards may reasonably be classed as part of the active circulation. Some money is lodged, at any moment, in "long hoards" because it has come into the hands of owners who choose to hold a part of their wealth in the form of money. Some is in "bear hoards" whose owners are waiting for a fall in bond and share prices to go back into the market.

Some bears, and some owners of wealth with a high preference for capital-certainty, hold bills rather than money. But it is natural to assume that, in the main, money is preferred to bills for long hoards because dealing in bills is a specialised business, for which many owners of long hoards have no inclination, and because it is not practicable in small sums. The advantage of money over bills for bear hoards is that it makes it possible to switch back into securities in less than three months, if that seems desirable, without the cost and the capital risk of switching into and out of bills.

Short hoards, long hoards, and bear hoards correspond to convenience, precaution, and speculation, mentioned by Keynes as motives for holding money.[1]

Now, the fall in interest rates which has occurred may slow down the active circulation somewhat. Money may idle a little longer in short hoards—the motive for economising balances is less[2]—but this effect will be slight, for the velocity of active circulation is fixed by fairly rigid habits. Thus, when there is an increase in money relative to national income, most of the new money cannot find a lodgement unless long or bear hoards are increased.[3]

The yields of all paper assets have fallen, and this in itself may lead some owners of wealth to prefer money. But the main effect is that the rise in the price of bonds and shares has enhanced the fear of a fall in their value

---

[1] *General Theory* [21], pp. 195–6. It is, of course, impossible to draw a hard and fast line between them. Convenience shades into precaution, and precaution would not give rise to a demand for money unless there was an element of speculation present. Cf. Fellner [5], p. 147.

[2] Mr. Kalecki ([17], p. 32) suggests that it is only the short rate which is relevant here. But surely this is a mistake. If an individual (or a firm) decides to economise balances in order to enjoy interest he is just as likely to put the money into bonds as bills. See also Kaldor [15], p. 14.

[3] Mr. Kaldor seems to deny that hoarding ever occurs ([15], p. 13, footnote), but on closer examination his argument appears to be purely verbal, as he calls deposits money only if they are in active circulation.

in the future, and so set a bearish movement on foot. Money, we have supposed, is usually preferred to bills for bear hoarding; if, however, some of the bears prefer bills, the bill rate is reduced all the more, and there is a further movement over the bill frontier into money.

Thus the result of increasing the quantity of money is to lower the short rate and to pull the long rate below its expected value to the point where the combined effect of these two movements increases hoards by the amount of the increase in the quantity of money.[1] (If the fall in interest rates induces an increase in national income, of course, part of the new money is required for active circulation, and the interest rates will not fall so far.)

A fall in national income relative to the stock of money (abstracting from a consequent change in expectations) has effects similar to the above. A reduction in the quantity of money or rise in national income has the converse effects.

To summarise: given the state of expectations, the long and short rates of interest both fall as the quantity of money increases relatively to national income. The fall in the short rate is steeper than the fall in the long,[2] so that the gap between the two increases with the quantity of money. The less the uncertainty (the more confident and unanimous the market that a departure of the rate of interest from its average value will quickly be reversed), the smaller is the response of the rates of interest to changes in the quantity of money, and the smaller is the gap between the two rates. In the limit, if the market confidently

[1] If the above is correct, it is misleading to say that the short rate is determined by demand and supply of money while the long rate is determined by the expected future short rate, for one of the main determinants of the demand for money is expectations about the course of the long rate itself.

[2] Unless uncertainty is so great that expectations about the future price of bonds have no influence at all upon the long rate.

believes that it knows that from tomorrow the rate of interest will be at its past average value, the long and the short rate will be equal to that value today. (In this case liquidity preference in Keynes' sense is absolute.)

So far we have been discussing the situation at a moment of time, with given expectations, but time marches on. We have supposed that expectations of the future interest rates depend upon past experience. When the bond rate is below its past average, expectations tend to be revised as time goes by, and the demand for money tends gradually to fall, but this is a slow process, and before it has had time to produce any effect all sorts of changes occur. Thus uncertainty is kept alive by the chances of history.

It has been objected against this theory that it leaves the rate of interest hanging by its own boot straps.[1] But there is no escape from the fact that the price today of any

[1] Both Mr. Hicks (*Value and Capital* [12], p. 164) and Mr. Kaldor ([15], p. 12) display a lively horror of boot straps, but it is not clear how they propose to escape from them. The view that the long rate can be determined solely from expectations about the short rate is untenable. It is true, in a world in which expectations are definite and unanimous, that when we know today's bond rate and today's bill rate, we can reckon what change in the price of bonds is expected over the life of the bills. Then, looking into a further future, we can assume that the bill rate then expected to rule is known, and that by then the expected price of bonds is expected to obtain. Then we can reckon the expected change in bond prices over the further future, and so on to Kingdom Come. Then the whole pattern of expectations could be described in terms of the expected short rates alone. But all this means is that rational expectations must be self-consistent. It certainly does not detach the rate of interest from dependence on its boot straps for, in such a world, the only reason for a difference between short and long rates is the expectation of a change in the long rate. Indeed, one might say that the short rate is simply an expression of expectations about bond prices. Moreover, the conception of expectations without uncertainty plunges us into philosophical difficulties (see above).

Professor Robertson ([32], p. 25) appears to hold (though he states positively only what he does *not* hold) that the long rate is determined partly by the "real forces" and partly by beliefs about how the real forces are going to behave in the future. But, if so, with these beliefs he has admitted a

long-lived object with low carrying costs is strongly influenced by expectations about what its price will be in the future. If the rate of interest is hanging by its boot straps, so is the price of Picasso's paintings.

We have very little knowledge of the influences shaping expectations. Past experience is no doubt the major element in expectations, but experience, as far as one can judge, is compounded in the market with a variety of theories and superstitions and the whole amalgam is played upon from day to day by the influences (including the last bank chairman's speech) which make up what Keynes called "the state of the news". Any theory that is widely believed tends to verify itself, so that there is a large element of "thinking makes it so" in the determination of interest rates.[1] This is all the more true when short-term speculation is prevalent.

A speculator has not the same attitude as an owner of wealth to liquidity, income-uncertainty, or capital-uncertainty. He is concerned with making money by forestalling changes in prices from day to day by "anticipating what average opinion expects the average opinion to be."[2]

Trojan horse full of expectations and liquidity preference into the citadel of the real forces.

In Mr. Kalecki's system expectations about the long rate, based on past experience, are a separate determinant of today's rate, and the system here set out is broadly the same as his (except for the point made above, p. 142, note 2) and owes a great deal to it.

My chief debt is to some pregnant hints to be found in Mr. Harrod's *Dynamic Economics* [8], see especially p. 62.

[1] This gives the "real forces" one more card of entry (cf. above, p. 139). If it is widely believed that, for example, an increase in the rate of investment raises the rate of interest, then the appearance of any symptom which is taken to indicate that investment is going to increase will have a tendency to raise interest rates.

[2] *General Theory* [21], p. 156. In reality, of course, there can be no quite clear-cut demarcation between speculators and owners of wealth who take a view about future prices, and the two classes shade into each other at the edges.

So long as the great bulk of transactions is made by owners of wealth and dealers in credit, the speculator has to guess how they will behave. The effect of speculation is then to speed up the movement of today's prices towards expected future prices. But, as soon as speculators become an important influence in the market, their business is to speculate on each other's behaviour. The market then becomes unstable, and falls into the condition described by Keynes under that misleading chapter heading, "The State of Long-Term Expectations".[1] The operations of the speculators cast a thick fog over future prospects for the owners of wealth, increase uncertainty all round, and so raise the general level of interest rates.

They also create a fog for the economist describing the capital market, which very much reduces the cogency of the above type of analysis, and totally deprives it of utility as a source of tips.

4. An Increase in the Rate of Investment

Abstracting from speculation (for if we do not, there is little to be said) we will now examine the effects of an increase in the rate of investment (say, induced by an improvement in prospective profits) which increases national income but does not go far enough to hit full employment and create inflationary conditions. If the banking system follows the policy of meeting the needs of trade, interest rates are held constant. To make the story interesting we will assume that the quantity of money is not altered.

Investment plans must be made before any actual outlay takes place. If entrepreneurs proceed by issuing shares

[1] *General Theory* [21], chapter XII.

before they begin to place orders for new capital goods, and hold money in short hoards for the time being, there is an increase in demand for money relatively to the supply and an increase in supply of shares relatively to demand, and the interest rates rise before the actual investment begins.[1] It is more natural to suppose, however, that entrepreneurs take bank advances as required and retire them by the issue of shares after the investment has been under way for some time.

Possible cases offer an endless variety of patterns. To simplify, we will assume that investment remains steady at the new higher rate during the period that we are discussing, that all investment is financed in the same way, and that it is financed by taking over-drafts which are repaid by issuing securities at a certain interval after they have been drawn upon. With these assumptions, while the investment continues there is a certain volume of bank advances outstanding at any moment, and the supply of securities keeps pace with the addition to wealth due to saving, after an initial wobble, which may go either way according as the issue of securities begins before or after the pattern of saving has become adjusted to the new rate of investment.

We will abstract from the gradual effect of a rise in the proportions of shares to total wealth, and consider only the immediate influences upon interest rates coming from the change in the rate of investment.

Let us compare a date in Period II, when the multiplier has run its course and national income has settled at the level appropriate to the new higher rate of investment, with a date in Period I, when investment was being carried out at the old rate.

[1] See Keynes, "Alternative Theories of the Rate of Interest" [19], *Economic Journal*, June 1937.

There is now a larger national income, and a larger demand for money in active circulation, including a swollen demand for short hoards, corresponding to the higher level at which saving is running.[1] Entrepreneurs have taken bank advances, and the banks sold out bills, so that the short rate has risen. Bond rates, as usual, have risen in sympathy.

The rise in interest rates puts a brake on the rise in demand for money by increasing the velocity of active circulation; at the same time it has drawn money out of bear and long hoards. The rates of interest have risen to the point where equilibrium is restored at the frontiers around money.

What has happened to shares? The same cause which induces the increase in investment—a rise in prospective profits—gives rise to better and more confident expectations of future dividends. For the time being, at least, the optimism which started investment off appears justified, for profits are in fact ruling higher while investment goes on. The price of shares has therefore risen at least sufficiently to keep yields at the level corresponding to the rate on bonds. (If we allow speculators out of the cage where we are keeping them assumed away, the price of shares may rise to any extent, and the normal relationship between bond and share yields may be reversed.) If this were all, share yields would move sympathetically with the bond rate—that is to say, they would be raised slightly by the increase in demand for money. But there is a further effect. With greater confidence in future profits, credit is improved and the risk attached to shares is felt to be reduced. Different shares will be differently affected.

---

[1] Professor Fellner ([5], p. 149) suggests that hoards held by entrepreneurs fall as general confidence increases. If this effect were to predominate, the rates of interest would normally fall as investment increases.

On the very "good" ones, for which the risk premium is in any case small, the yield will have risen in sympathy with bonds; on others, particularly those whose firms are taking the biggest part in the industrial boom, it will have fallen. Lumping all shares together, their yield, on balance, is most likely to be reduced.

Our interest rates now stand thus, at a date in Period II compared to Period I: The short rate is higher. Bond rates are higher than in Period I (but not by much) and share rates are likely to be lower.

The yield on existing paper assets has a strong influence on the cost of new borrowing. Concerns which borrow at near the gilt-edged rate will find borrowing a little dearer and may be inclined to defer investment plans (though it is more likely that, in the general atmosphere of optimism, they will take the rise in their stride). Industrialists in the main find borrowing easier. The improved prospect of profit counts twice over—once in promoting investment at a given cost of borrowing and once in lowering the cost of borrowing.[1]

Keynes himself makes this point,[2] but the habit of thinking in terms of *the* rate of interest led him to overlook the fact that the most relevant interest rate is likely to be falling when investment is increasing, and to make the quite unnecessary concession to classical ideas that the movement in interest rates which accompanies a boom sets a drag upon the increase in investment.

[1] This argument has not much force in the case of a large established firm, for which there need not be any close connection between the timing of borrowing and of investment, but there is much investment which cannot be undertaken until finance for it has been secured.

[2] *General Theory* [21], p. 158.

5. An Increase in Thriftiness

We may now consider the much debated question of the effect of thriftiness on the rate of interest.[1] Our discussion of the "real forces" implied that, in a very broad sense and a very long run, a high state of thriftiness relative to investment opportunities helps to keep interest rates low. In so far as it does so, accumulation of real capital may be greater than it would have been if interest rates had been higher, though not necessarily greater than it would have been if thriftiness had been less. In what follows we are not concerned with such long-run considerations, but with examining the impact of an increase in thriftiness upon interest rates in a very short and in a medium run.

Let us suppose that the thriftiness of our community has increased, which shows itself in the first instance in a reduction in the rate of outlay for consumption goods by some section of the public. We will first consider how the situation would develop *if* planned investment were unaffected, and then re-examine the influence of what has happened upon investment plans. It simplifies exposition if we postulate that the rate of planned investment is zero, but this means only that sentences such as "the stock of capital is unchanged" are substituted for "the stock of capital is the same as it would have been if this had not happened," and so forth. We must divide time up into periods, not necessarily of the same length. Period I is the time before the change occurred. In Period II consumption is lower than in Period I by the amount of the designed increase of saving but nothing else has had time to alter. Stocks have piled up in the shops. If we value the stocks at full retail prices, including the retailers' profit,

[1] Cf. Robertson [32], pp. 18 et seq.

we may say that national income is unchanged. At the end of Period II *ex-post* saving has occurred equal to the undesigned rise in stocks. In Period III (which is likely to be longer than II) retailers reduce purchases, the fall in national income works its way through the system, and there will be a secondary decline in consumption on top of the first. Stocks have to be reduced to the level appropriate to the new rate of consumption, so that there will be an extra fall in income and fall in employment while the redundant stocks of Period I and the undesigned accumulation of Period II are worked off. In Period IV disinvestment in stocks has come to an end, there is a recovery of employment relatively to Period III, and we settle down to a new position of short-period equilibrium with a lower level of consumption appropriate to the now higher thriftiness and the unchanged rate of investment.

How have the rates of interest been behaving? Let us place ourselves at the point of time where Period II ends. We find members of the public with an increment of wealth compared to their position in Period I. There are a great many possible consequences in the financial sphere. Let us pick out two simple cases:

(1) The savers are holding short hoards, equal to their increment of wealth, which they have not yet placed in securities.
(2) They have already purchased bonds.

Retailers have acquired real assets to the value of the undesigned increase in stocks. Part of this value is represented by profits which they have failed to realise. According to the convention we have adopted of calling the national income constant, the missing profits must be regarded as savings which the retailers have, willy-nilly, invested in stocks. The rest of the value of stocks represents outgoings which they would normally have paid out of receipts, and for which they now require finance. This division of the value of the stocks into two parts complicates the argument. At first we will abstract from it by assuming that the retailers finance the whole value of the stocks in the same way. Methods of finance vary greatly according to the way business is conducted. Again we may pick out a few simple cases from amongst all the possibilities:

(a) The retailers have run down cash balances.
(b) They have taken bank advances.
(c) They have sold bonds which they were formerly holding.

Combining (1) with (a), cash released from retailers' balances matches the increase in cash held by savers, and nothing alters. Combining (2) with (c), the retailers sell bonds equivalent to those that the savers buy, and again nothing alters. Combining (1) with (c), the savers hoard money and the retailers sell bonds. The demand for money has increased, which raises interest rates in the converse of the manner described above. Besides this, the demand for bonds has fallen, which tends to increase the gap between long and short rates. Combining (2) with (a), the savers have bought bonds and the retailers have parted with money. The rates of interest fall, and the gap between them tends to narrow.

In case (b) the banks have made advances and, since the quantity of money is assumed constant, they have sold out bills. This raises the short rate of interest, and the long rate tends to rise in sympathy. If we combine this with case (1) (savers holding money), the increase in demand for money reinforces the rise in interest rates. If we combine it with (2) (savers holding bonds), the increase in demand for bonds tends to counteract it.

In so far as the various types of case occur together they tend to offset each others' effects upon the interest rates.

Slight differences are introduced if we take account of the retailers' missing profits. Suppose that their savings in Period I exceeded the missing profits, and that their personal expenditure is the same in Period II as in Period I; then, in the case which combines (1) and (a), the absorption of cash by savers is equal to the full value of the undesigned accumulation of stocks, while the release of cash by retailers which finances them is short of the full value by the amount of the missing profits. There is thus a net increase in demand for money, and the interest rates rise. And so on.

But the argument has grown tedious. Its upshot is that in Period II the effect upon interest rates is not likely to be large, and, in so far as there is an effect, it may go either way.

Let us now jump over the turbid eddies of Period III and place ourselves at a point of time some way along in Period IV, when things have settled down.

Still assuming, provisionally, that planned investment is unchanged at zero, we have a national income lower than that in Period I by the reduced consumption of the first group of savers *plus* the reduction brought about by the secondary decline in incomes and employment in accordance with the multiplier. A smaller amount of money is required in active circulation than in Period I. Bank advances have been paid off and (assuming a constant quantity of money) the short rate of interest is lower than in Period I. No net investment has taken place; therefore there has been zero *ex-post* saving over the period as a whole (neglecting the effect of disinvestment in stocks and working capital owing to the fall in the level of output), so that the total of outstanding assets and the total of privately owned wealth are unchanged. Abstracting from any change in expectations about the long rate of interest owing to the experiences of the transition period, there has been a fall in the bond rate, in sympathy with the short rate. The consumption trades are doing badly compared to Period I, and shares are likely to be adversely affected. On the very "good" ones the yield may move in sympathy with the fall in bond and short rates, but many will suffer from a rise in riskiness, owing to poor prospects of profit in the consumption trades. Thus our picture is: a lower short rate in Period IV compared to I, a slightly lower bond and best share rate, and a higher yield of shares in general.

This pattern of interest rates does not look very encouraging to investment, and it seems that our provisional assumption of a constant rate of investment must be revised in the downward direction because of the surplus capacity and low profits in the consumption trades and the high cost of industrial borrowing.

6. A CHEAP MONEY POLICY

The last case we will examine is a cheap money policy. A campaign by the monetary authorities to lower interest rates to counter unemployment, if successful, will stimulate activity. Undertaken in a situation which is already inflationary, it will necessitate stronger anti-inflation measures (such as a larger budget surplus). We are not here concerned with discussing its effectiveness in the first case, or its advisability in the second, but merely to study the mechanics of its operation. This story necessarily depends very much upon its institutional and political setting. The following reflects the English scene as far as our stylised picture of the capital market permits.

The first move in the campaign is for the Central Bank to dose the banks with cash, by open market purchases. The amount of advances the banks can make is limited by the demand from good borrowers. The demand is very inelastic (though it shifts violently up and down with the state of trade), so the banks, between whom competition is highly imperfect, see no advantage in cheapening their price. The redundant cash reserve must go into bills. Any rate of return is better than none. The banks with redundant cash find themselves in much the same position as a group of firms with surplus capacity and zero prime costs. If perfect competition prevailed, the bill rate would go to next to nothing and the banks could not cover their costs. They therefore fix up a gentleman's agreement which keeps the bill rate steady at a low level. The bill rate is maintained at this low level by the Central Bank's giving another dose of cash whenever it threatens to rise.

If the Central Bank is operating in the old orthodox manner, its power ends here, and the authorities must rely on the dealers in credit to bring the long rates down. Nowadays the authorities reinforce the action of the banking system by going into the bond market directly. If necessary, they issue bills in order to buy bonds, the quantity of money being adjusted to whatever level is required to keep the bill rate at its bottom stop. The low interest rates may slow down the velocity of active circulation so that money, as the saying is, stagnates in pools. Long hoards are swollen by the fall in the current rates and bear hoards by the fact that expected future rates are not yet revised.

As time goes by, experience of a long rate that is persistently somewhat lower than the expected rate lowers the expected rate and so lowers the actual rate further. The yield on shares falls in sympathy with the bond rates. Thus the whole complex of rates gradually falls through time. If the authorities take it gently and do not try to push the rate down too fast, and if they stick consistently to the policy, once begun, so that the market never has the experience of today's rate being higher than yesterday's, it is hard to discern any limit to the possible fall in interest rates (except the mere technical costs of dealing) so long as the full-employment interest rate is below the actual level of rates or is held below it by a budget surplus or other means.

All goes smoothly so long as the authorities are working with the grain of market opinion[1]. But if they embark on the policy and begin to buy bonds at a time when the long rate is generally expected to rise, they come sharply into conflict with market opinion. So long as the expected rate remains high, they have to go on holding bonds and supplying money for bear hoards. If they persist resolutely, a moment will come when the bears are convinced that the new low rate has come to stay. Money then moves out of bear hoards into bonds, and the authorities can gradually sell off to ex-bears the bonds they have been holding, retire bills, and reduce the quantity of money to the level which will just hold the bill rate at its bottom stop.

But if the authorities' nerves are shaken by the ferocious growls with which the bears have been deafening them all this time, and once allow bond prices to relapse, the growling of the bears turns to joyous yelps of "I told you so" and the expected future bond rate is so much the higher for ever after.

[1] Cf. *General Theory* [21], p. 203.

INDEX OF REFERENCES

1. Bauer, P., and Yamey, B. S., "Economic Progress and Occupational Distribution", *Economic Journal*, December 1951. . . 44

2. Domar, E. D., "Expansion and Employment," *American Economic Review*, March 1947. 25, 129

3. Duesenberry, J. S., *Income, Saving and the Theory of Consumer Behaviour*. 35

4. *Economics Committee, Papers of the Royal Commission on Population*, Vol. III. . . . 40

5. Fellner, W. J., *Monetary Policies and Full Employment*. 146, 150, 156

6. Graaff, J. de V., "Mr. Harrod on Hump Saving", *Economica*, February 1950. . . 55

6a. Goodwin, R. M., "Econometrics in Business-Cycle Analysis," Chapter 22 of Hansen, *Business Cycles and Natural Income* . . 61

7. Hahn, F. H., "A Recent Contribution to Trade Cycle Theory", *Quarterly Review, Banca Nazionale del Lavoro*, December 1950. 132

8. Harrod, R. F., *Towards a Dynamic Economics*. 10 25, 55, 56, 97, 129 et seq.

9. Hicks, J. R., *A Contribution to the Theory of the Trade Cycle*. . . . 35, 60, 61, 132

10. Hicks, J. R., "Mr. Keynes and the Classics", *Econometrica*, April 1937. 7

11. Hicks, J. R., *The Theory of Wages*. . 99, 100

12. Hicks, J. R., *Value and Capital.* . . . 152

13. Hicks, J. R., "World Recovery after the War", *Economic Journal*, June 1947. . . . 12

14. Kaldor, N., "A Model of the Trade Cycle", *Economic Journal*, March 1940. . . 61

15. Kaldor, N., "Speculation and Economic Stability", *Review of Economic Studies*, October 1939. . . . 9, 142, 150, 152

16. Kalecki, M., *Essays in the Theory of Economic Fluctuations.* 17, 18, 37, 56, 61, 63, 86, 129

17. Kalecki, M., *Studies in Economic Dynamics.* 142, 150 42, 61, 153

18. Keirstead, B. S., *The Theory of Economic Change.* 37, 71, 100

19. Keynes, J. M., "Alternative Theories of the Rate of Interest", *Economic Journal*, June 1937 155

20. Keynes, J. M., *Essays in Persuasion.*. . . 56

21. Keynes, J. M., *The General Theory of Employment, Interest and Money.* ix, 3, 7, 60, 141, 148, 150, 153, 154, 156, 164

22. Keynes, J. M., *A Treatise on Money*. 130, 133, 148

23. Luxemburg, Rosa., *The Accumulation of Capital* (trans. Agnes Schwarzschild).25,30,117,126 et seq.

24. Marshall, A., "Evidence before the Committee on India Currency." *Official Papers*. . . 124

25. Marshall, A., *Principles of Economics*, seventh edition. . . . 3, 4, 120 et seq.

26. Marshall, A., *The Pure Theory of Domestic Values.* 125

27. Marx, K., *Capital.* Vols. II and III (trans. E. Untermann). . . 26, 58, 115 et seq.

28. Modigliani, F., "Liquidity Preference and the Theory of Interest and Money", *Econometrica*, January 1944. . . . . 5, 7, 9

29. Pigou, A. C., *The Economics of Welfare*, fourth edition 100

30. Pigou, A. C., *Lapses from Full Employment.* . 7

31. Pigou, A. C., "Real and Money Wage Rates", *Economic Journal*, September 1937. . . 7

32. Robertson, D. H., *Essays in Monetary Theory.* 14, 138, 139, 152, 158

33. Robertson, D. H., *A Study of Industrial Fluctuations.* 58

34. Robinson, Joan, "The Classification of Inventions", *Review of Economic Studies*, February 1938. . . . . 86, 102

35. Robinson, Joan, *Essays in the Theory of Employment*, second edition. . . 57, 64, 96

36. Robinson, Joan, *An Essay on Marxian Economics.* 120

37. Rostow, W. W., "Some Notes on Mr. Hicks and History", *American Economic Review*, June 1951. 72

38. Samuelson, P., "The Evaluation of Real National Income", *Oxford Economic Papers*, January 1950. 5

39. Samuelson, P., *Foundations of Economic Analysis.* 133

40. Schelling, T. C., "Capital Growth and Equilibrium", *American Economic Review*, December 1947. . . . . 26, 130

41. Schumpeter, *Capitalism, Socialism and Democracy.* 36

42. Shackle, G. L. S., *Expectations in Economics*.   146

43. Shove, G. F., "Mrs. Robinson on Marxian Economics", *Economic Journal*, April 1944. 122, 125

44. Shove, G. F., "The Place of Marshall's *Principles* in the Development of Economic Theory", *Economic Journal*, December 1942   121

45. Sraffa, P., "The Laws of Returns under Competitive Conditions", *Economic Journal*, December 1926.   121

46. Stern, E. H., "Capital Requirements in Progressive Economies", *Economica*, August 1945.   37

47. Tinbergen, J., *The Dynamics of Business Cycles*.   132

48. Wicksell, K., *Interest and Prices* (trans. R. F. Kahn).   124

49. Wicksteed P., *The Co-ordination of the Laws of Distribution*.   6

50. Yamey, B. S., *see* Bauer.

GENERAL INDEX